MAKING AND KEEPING
LIFETIME RELATIONSHIPS

HOW TO BE A
BEST FRIEND
FOREVER

DR. JOHN TOWNSEND

Best-selling Author of *Boundaries*—2 Million Copies Sold

Dedication

To anyone who believes
in the life-sustaining value of best friends.

Contents

Acknowledgments

Sealy Yates, my literary agent: Your involvement in every aspect of this book is deeply appreciated.

Byron Williamson, publisher, Worthy Publishing: Thanks for your inexhaustible creative energy and friendship.

Jeana Ledbetter, vice president of editorial, Worthy Publishing: When you are part of a book, it's always a much better book.

Rob Birkhead, senior vice president of marketing, Worthy Publishing: Your graphic and artistic excellence is transformative to this content.

Kris Bearss, executive editor, Worthy Publishing: Your supervision of the book has made a great, positive difference.

Angela Scheff, my editor: Thanks for all the hours of helping craft the ideas into a form that would engage and help the reader.

Barbi, my wife: Thanks for spending so much time thinking through the material with me.

Introduction:
Lifelines

Recently, I was having lunch with some friends when the topic turned to friendship itself. I had been researching the subject for a while, so I threw out an open-ended question: "How important have your best friends been for you?" I was simply doing some informal information gathering. There was a brief silence before people gave the following ideas about friends:

- They have been safe places where I can be myself.
- They are a few people I can be comfortable with.
- They are the ones I go to when I need support.
- They know and accept all of me.
- They have walked with me through my marriage and childrearing years.

- I have found God in a deeper way through these relationships.
- They have helped me through tough times.
- They have made my life more meaningful.

The answers were all thoughtful and positive—and fairly predictable. They probably represent what any of us would say about our closest friendships. Then one woman, who I had not known for long and who had been silent until this point, said: "I probably wouldn't be here without them."

I heard something in her voice, so I asked, "You mean, you probably would not be where you are these days in life—that sort of thing?"

She looked directly at me. "No. I probably wouldn't be here. *Here* here. On earth."

I felt the level of the conversation change, as no one could have predicted that answer. We were in a whole new and deeper arena with that one thought. The speaker, Rachel, was not someone you would think of as being in a crisis or having experienced a great deal of trauma. She was a professional in her mid-forties, married, with two children.

I then asked her to share her story with us. She told us about years of serious and painful struggles: an abusive childhood, a nightmare of a first marriage, and, by far most difficult of all, the death of one of her children. That last event, she said, almost put her under. When I asked how she got through these massive losses, she said, "God and three friends." God, she said, sustained and guided her through the very dark years. And three friends—three *best friends*—were there in so many ways: They listened to Rachel. They supported her. They stayed at the hospital during her child's illness. They let her feel whatever she needed to feel about her life. They lent her money when her job fell through. They drove her to church and to her therapist's office when she could hardly move. "That's what I meant about saying that without them, I probably wouldn't be here," Rachel told us.

More Vital Than You Can Imagine

I begin with this story because it illustrates a problem we have in our best friendships: the word *friends* has somehow been robbed of its meaning and power. It has been diluted. Friends, especially best friends, are often explained in a vanilla way, in the same manner you would say, "We just decided to stay in for the evening and watch some reruns." There is nothing wrong with that, and it can be a good experience. Likewise, friendships can appear comfortable, safe—and not much more than that. But Rachel does not see it that way, and I agree with her. She sees her best friends as a lifeline. Her three relationships were not simply helpful and encouraging. They were critical. They were a matter of survival. I think that is more of what friendships should be about: people we go to with our deepest dreams, needs, and questions, and who are lifelines to us. People who bring us life.

As I work with people and organizations, I have noticed several reasons that the power and meaning of friendships have been diluted in our present-day experience. One is that many people are simply isolated in the first place and, though they want more close relationships, they've learned to live without them. They may have trust issues or painful past relationships, but whatever the reason, they are lonely even though they are surrounded by people. Others are simply not aware of their deeper need. In their experience, it is enough to have pleasant and positive conversations with others and not much more. They feel bad for people who struggle, but have not experienced "dark night of the soul" seasons, or seasons of great celebration for that matter, that would drive them to share with others. Some people don't possess the required skills and abilities to deepen a relationship. Still others put their friendship energy almost exclusively into the opposite sex, either in dating or marriage, and have difficulty experiencing high levels of need for nonromantic friends. They are stuck in a couple's world, which can exclude the idea of best friends. In addition, some people have difficulty opening up to anyone but their close family members. Nonfamily friends just do not make it into the circle. There are other reasons, but however it plays out, friendships—especially best friendships—don't bring to us what they were intended to bring.

Jesus saw friends as central in a way that we often miss. He told his disciples that he was going to stop calling them his servants and change things: "Instead, I have called you friends, for everything that I learned from my Father I have made known to you" (John 15:15). He was making a distinction between two types of relationships: servants and friends are very different. You give a directive to a servant. But you bring a friend into your confidence. At lunch, you tell the waiter you'd like a refill on your coffee, and he does it. But you tell a friend that you need that refill because you didn't get a lot of sleep last night with a sick child at home. You make known to your friend what is going on in your life.

In addition, at the end of Jesus' life, during his time of deep trouble and distress while he was praying at Gethsemane, Jesus asked his three closest friends—Peter, James, and John—to keep watch with him (Mark 14:32–34). Imagine God himself asking three friends to support him! It seems so dependent of Jesus, so "unspiritual." The stereotype is that he should have only looked to his heavenly Father for support. But the reality is that Jesus modeled a need for both divine and human connections.

I think most of us are missing out in our best friendships in these ways. We are more on the safe side, not the Rachel side, of things. And I hope that this book will help you to get the most out of what is available to you. Because when you have a few real best friends, and you know what to do with them, life can be significantly better, fuller, and richer.

We often don't have time or energy to make many BFs in life, so it's good to know how to make them count. (And when people say, "I have lots of best friends," it is the sign of someone who is not familiar with true and deep relationships.)

There are many examples of famous best friendships, both in history and currently: David and Jonathan. Roosevelt and Churchill. Lewis and Tolkien. Sinatra and Martin. Damon and Affleck. Oprah and Gayle. We have a fascination with the dynamics of these relationships, partially because the people are well known, and partially because we want long-lasting and safe relationships like these.

Unused Potential

Most of us aren't experiencing the highest level of good that is available from our friendships. You may find a great deal of warmth, understanding, encouragement, and shared life experiences in your best friendships. But I believe that for most of us, there can be much more richness, growth, and fulfillment as well. Think about all the important areas of your life, and how you are intentional about growth and improvement:

- The gym for your body
- Church for your spiritual life
- Training for your career
- Marriage seminars for you and your spouse
- Parenting workshops for your family
- Financial training for your money
- Classes for your sports and hobbies

However, we don't tend to pay a great deal of attention to being more intentional about our friendships. We aren't prone to focus on our best friends and on making those relationships even better. Think for a moment about those few special people on your BF list and ask yourself these two questions:

1. *If this relationship is a good one, would it be worth the exploration to make it a great one?* If you like the person and are drawn to her, why not? You are BFs for a reason. There is good you are both experiencing today as you walk through life. Why not more and better?

2. *Are there specific areas of life in which my best friends and I could do better for each other?* Some friendships tend to be "specialty" relationships. That is, the energy stays on parenting, marriage, or dating, and doesn't delve into physical health, family of origin, spiritual values, or finances. While each BF does have its area of specialty, there may be untapped help available in your relationship.

I have experienced the "problem of potential" in my own friendships and have seen great results in applying the principles I've learned. I had lunch recently with a close friend, where we told each other that we were important to each other in specific ways. It was something I think we both were aware of, but had never been clear about. We each left the conversation with a deep sense of "This person is a lifer for me." The very talk we had helped us use more of the potential in the relationship.

The closest thing to this kind of thinking is in the romantic sphere of life—marriage and dating—where there is a lot of good research and helpful principles for creating intimacy, communication, and depth within those relationships. While the romantic world should certainly also offer you a close friendship, that is only one person. The friendship world should consist of several people and ideally include your partner. That arena has its own ideas and principles, found in this book, that can enrich and fulfill your relationships in a unique way.

A Necessity

You may have a healthy marriage or dating relationship. But whatever is going on in your life, the research keeps pointing to the conclusion that *all aspects of our lives are deeply affected by the presence or absence of friendships.* Friendships are more than a luxury or icing on the cake. They are a necessity.

Researchers have been studying the effects of social isolation since the 1970s, and the evidence is overwhelming. They have found that when people are disconnected from relationships, their medical and psychological conditions suffer.[1] Friendships even affect our finances. A recent long-term study found that during high school, if you were named as a close friend by someone else, you were likely to make 2 percent more income later in life. This study discovered a multiplier effect as well: being named by five people equaled a 10 percent increase in wages.[2]

The flow of scientific data supports what the Bible says about friendships:

> Two are better than one, because they have a good return for their work: If one falls down, his friend can help him up. But pity the man who falls and has no one to help him up.
>
> Also, if two lie down together, they will keep warm. But how can one keep warm alone? Though one may be overpowered, two can defend themselves. A cord of three strands is not quickly broken. (Ecclesiastes 4:9–12)

Can you relate to "falling down" in life and not having someone you can trust deeply to talk to about it? When we fall down alone, it takes much more effort to get back up in life again.

FRIENDSHIP'S ORIGIN AND PURPOSE

Friendships are actually an essential part of our childhood development. Infants don't start life looking for buddies. They come into the world looking for a life-support system called Mother. That is their first and most primary relationship, where they begin to experience how to connect, trust, and reach out. This prepares them for all other relationships. They find that relationship is the best place to be, and life goes better when they are in a connection. At that point, they are able to then make contact with Dad, and, after that, brothers and sisters.

After that, between ages four and eleven, kids gradually become more and more interested and involved with friendships. Their early experiences with the family have given them the readiness to leave those first relationships and venture out into the social world, part of the "leaving and cleaving" process designed by God (see Genesis 2:24 KJV). This is when school, playdates, sports, the arts, and church relationships flourish.

The child's social relationships often begin to compete with the family, and parents have to establish age-appropriate balances to keep it all in place. It is common for parents to feel as though their kids don't see home as special anymore. But if home base is a good, warm, and structured place, it is often a sign that the family has done its job well.

The "friendship explosion," then, must make room for puberty and romantic interests, starting at around twelve years of age. At this point, there is a confusing time of integrating romantic relationships with same-sex and opposite-sex friendships, which continues into the twenties. All this helps prepare the young person ultimately for grown-up activities such as establishing a mature support system, dating, marriage, and parenting. The end result is a healthy blend of romantic and nonromantic relationships, which provide the connectedness and growth we need.

This entire process is a shift in the center of our lives, from what is called our "family of origin" to our own friends and new families. As part of that leaving and cleaving, friends are more and more the sources of love, care, direction, and interest for us. The family of origin, if it's a loving and healthy one, is part of this, but can no longer be the center of it. That is the grand design: to let young people take what they have learned from their families and spread their wings and apply it to their new lives. In that sense, friends are our "second family." They continue our growth and development as we mature: emotionally, relationally, spiritually, and professionally. They also provide what ingredients of growth might have been lacking in our family of origin, or help us heal from what might have been injured there as well.

Jesus referred to the second family in his own life experience:

Then Jesus' mother and brothers arrived. Standing outside, they sent someone in to call him. A crowd was sitting around him, and they told him, "Your mother and brothers are outside looking for you." "Who are my mother and my brothers?" he asked. Then he looked at those seated in a circle around him and said, "Here are my mother and my brothers! Whoever does God's will is my brother and sister and mother." (Mark 3:31–35)

In other words, those who have deeply shared like values toward God are the family we need as adults. Friends become family.

I was facilitating a small group of people who wanted to go deeper into their relationships with themselves, with God, and with each other. It was a vulnerable and intimate set of experiences, in which the members took big risks with each other and found a depth of friendship they had not had before. After several months of meetings, I asked for feedback on how the group was going. One of the members said, "This is how the body of Christ should be functioning."

As we talked, I realized that she was referring to all the "one anothers" the New Testament teaches, and how those should be norms for our best and highest relationships: be devoted, honor, live in harmony, don't pass judgment, accept, be patient, forgive, teach and admonish, spur to love and good deeds, and love deeply from the heart. This is how friendships should be. This is how family should be.

At the time of this writing, our sons have now entered college. My wife, Barbi, and I have had to continually adjust to the fact that our sons are much more outward-bound and friend-oriented than they are nest-oriented. We stay connected to the boys a great deal, but the energy is clearly "out there," where it needs to be.

In the same way, as a conference relationship speaker, I am privileged to talk to parents who have embraced their new role with their adult children. Though they will always be Mom and Dad, and share all the history, love, and honor that entails, they have accepted that they aren't the center of their kids' lives and have moved to the side, so to speak. It is not easy, and every parent must fight the urge to keep their teenagers and young adults totally based on the family. We have to let them go so that they can have great friendships like we should have in our own lives. They are learning how to be a good friend from the principles they pick up at home.

BEING A GOOD FRIEND

As a psychologist and relationship expert, I have observed people relating to each other for many years and have discovered some principles that will improve any best friend relationship. In my own life, I have found these same principles operating. I am fortunate to have my own set of BFFs who have been with me for years and walked through life with me. I can't imagine experiencing the world without them, and I am grateful to God and to them for that.

Not too long ago, I asked some of my closest friends if we could have a "friendship audit" and talk about us. It was a little awkward at first, especially with people I've known for several decades. How do you switch from "How's life?" to "How are we?" There's no smooth way to do this, so we just jumped in.

And I'm so glad we did. Each friend I talked with reported that they came away feeling closer to me and better about the relationship, and I did as well. In one friendship, what came up was the reality that we have always been there for each other, in good times and bad. In another, we acknowledged that we believe in the good we see in each other. In another, mutual respect for each other's lives was a major element of the relationship.

The good between us far outweighed the bad, which would make sense for a very close relationship. But that doesn't mean it was all affirmations and roses either. One friend said, "I have had to adjust my expectations downward with us." It was his nice way of saying that he thought I was doing a substandard job of calling and taking initiative to stay in touch. He was right: I was letting him do more of the work, and I felt remorse when he mentioned it. I hated that someone I value that much would feel that way. When a close friend gives a reality check like that, it has a deep impact. I told him I wanted to change and would like to be a better friend in that area.

Another friend said, "I hesitate to call you out of the blue sometimes because you seem really busy." There is a common thread between these two conversations, which is that I often get too tied up in what I do and don't make those important spontaneous calls as I should. We talked about that one: whether I put out a "Not Available" signal or whether he had difficulty taking risks, for what is the harm when a person says, "I can't talk right now"? We ultimately agreed that even though I am busy, I need this friend in my life, and if he calls, I would really welcome the call. If I couldn't talk or meet then, I would make sure we did sometime soon.

The pattern of me being less accessible to my friends than I would like to be was important to notice as well. If a couple of people you trust tell you something similar, pay attention. This is a gold mine of valuable information. Since I have received this feedback, I have taken time to reflect deeply on these behaviors and am making significant changes to make things better. It's good to know I have best friends I can trust to tell me if I'm changing or not!

I really value my friends and need them in my life. A Russian proverb says, "Tell me who's your friend and I'll tell you who you are." I hope that this book, and the ideas here, will help you to find out more about who you are by deepening your connections with your own best friends.

1

Fs, BFs, and BFFs

A friendship should add great things to your life: trust, companionship, and shared experiences, for example. But it will also cost you something: time, energy, and commitment. Even the most easygoing friendship requires some effort and investment. Given the energy involved, it leads to the question: should all BFs (best friends) also be BFFs (best friends forever)? Ideally, I think so. That depends on how life and circumstances go. Few things on this earth will last forever. But the second "F" in this title has to do more with the reality that the best friendships are open-ended about time and do not come with an expiration date. If we know that we will be moving to another town in a year, it will be hard to deeply engage with someone who lives there, though it is possible. So as you explore and engage in your relationship, you are most likely operating as though you will be BFFs.

FRIENDS

Let's understand our terms a bit here. A friend once told me, "I know so many people who make a BF out of someone they have known for a week, and there's something weird about that." While such a move is usually made due to a lack of information, or a crisis, or desperation, it is not how we are to develop friendships. We are to guard our hearts (Proverbs 4:23) and spend time and energy making sure anyone we let in our lives and hearts really deserves to have a place there. A BF is a kind of friend, so it is important to understand the "F" part of the word.

"Friend" is an extremely popular and broad term. When you read the checkout stand magazines, or google the word, it is a hard concept to pin down. Most of the descriptions are either very general or very anecdotal:

- Someone who shares life with you

- A person who accepts you as you are

- An individual you can say anything to and be anyone with

• Someone you look forward to sitting down with and talking about what you've been up to, as well as your joys and your struggles

These are descriptive, but they don't identify the essence of friendship in a way that presents clear lines about what it is and isn't.

After spending time researching this topic, I've come to the conclusion that at the DNA level, a friendship must have three elements: *knowing, liking,* and *presence.* These seem simple, but they are the three key components that are universal in friendships, from neighbors to church relationships to work connections.

1. *Knowing.* You have objective information and personal experience with the person. You know where they live, their marital and parental status, what they do for work, their hobbies, their faith. On a personal level, you may know their history, their likes and dislikes, and their dreams and hurts. *Knowing* provides the foundation of whether or not this relationship will be a friendship, and how deep it can go. And if what you know is scary or toxic, you need that information as well.

2. *Liking.* You want to spend time with each other. You are drawn to each other's presence. When life happens, for

good or bad, you want them to know about it, and you want to know about their life. You don't have to make yourself call or visit because you should, or because they are good for you. It's about a *want to*, not a *have to*. The *liking* aspect also helps when you have conflicts or problems in the relationship. It serves as an anesthetic to get over rough patches. And if you don't like someone, it is hard to call your relationship a friendship. A duty or a professional acquaintance or some sort of an obligation, maybe. But not a friendship.

3. *Presence.* Friends spend time together. That is how *knowing* and *liking* happen. It may be a phone call, a lunch, an evening, a bike ride, a vacation. But time together is essential. The more time together between two good people, the better the relationship. There is a mutual commitment to be with each other, and you gladly pay the price for its benefits. Sometimes people move away and don't see each other much. That doesn't mean they aren't friends, just that it is harder. But if the time was put in prior to the move, like making many deposits in an investment account, it is much easier to stay connected.

Think of your BFs now. You probably can recognize the presence of these three components in different amounts. But you have to have all three. They are the basics that define a friendship and also a best friendship.

BEST FRIENDS

Now to your best friendships, a special category. If a friendship is when someone has access to the information that is you, then best friendship is when you *hand over the key to the vault.* That is, you let the person know you at the deepest and most vulnerable level. You invite them in to what is most important to you, your

- Dreams
- Vision for Life
- Feelings
- Core values
- Strengths
- Hurts
- Secrets
- Sins
- Mistakes
- Past
- Heartaches

These are not easy things to let others in on. But they are essential for having close friends. Handing over the key to the vault means you are saying, in essence, *I entrust you with myself. Be safe for me and also help me be a better person.* Just as a bank vault contains precious investments, your personal vault is something to be both preserved safely, without condemnation, and also developed and grown over time into something much richer.

A friend of mine attended a coaching team I was leading for professional people. He signed up for business growth with a personal twist. He didn't know anyone on the team, yet a great deal of the time the team members spent with each other consisted of connection, honesty, and challenging each other to excellence. Over the months, he began developing relationships with these people, and he and his wife would go to dinner with other members and their spouses. The group became part of his normal network of friendships, as well as friends on a deeper level.

He didn't expect this to happen, nor did he plan for it. But their shared commitment drew him in and an atmosphere of knowing, liking, and presence was created. The same thing happens every day in casual friendships that grow, in small groups, and in specialty groups sharing common hobbies and interests.

A best friend, then, is not someone who has some mysterious and unfathomable special quality no one else has. Rather, she is someone who ideally has become a high-priority relationship for you that you will invest in personally. You will find yourself wanting to know her at even deeper levels. You'll find a growing and great well of love for her inside you, and become fiercely loyal to and protective of your time together, for it is vital to you both. That is the way it should work, and the way it works best.

BEST FRIENDS FOREVER

How do we know if a BF is really a BFF? When we use the word *forever*, we mean, "I don't see an end to this relationship." This is someone who is so important and special to me that they are in my Hall of Fame. This is a person who I want to be a permanent part of my life. I want their imprint on me, their stamp on me, their effect on me, with no end in sight. They are that significant to me.

ONE OR SEVERAL?

Is there room for only one BF, or can there be more than one? Some people believe this is a one-person arrangement, that a best friend means a number one friend. While we can have a closest friend, this is not always the way it is. "Best" simply indicates that a few relationships run deepest in your life and commitment. It is similar to best movies, restaurants, and sports teams.

The reality is also that we need more than one person to

enhance the quality of our life and relationships. Different friends have different strengths that bring out different qualities. Variety helps. It is a good thing to be able to call several people "my best friends," and it is a good goal to move toward.

A woman I was counseling began to pay close attention to her best friendships, seeing how much of a difference they made in her quality of life. She made the discovery that one BF had the ability to draw her out, be vulnerable, and go deep about the emotional areas of life. She loved how her friend was able to be there for her, and it meant a great deal to her. At the same time, however, she had another friend who showed her love and care by practical means: advice, good ideas, financial help, and suggestions. Their conversations had a different tone, but the value was there, just the same. "BF" is a plural term.

Male or Female?

What about opposite-sex best friends? I hear this question a great deal. Many people are concerned that a close opposite-sex relationship is too dangerous because of the possibility that emotional intimacy will end up being acted out sexually. So, by that reasoning, we should limit our deeper friendships to the same sex.

There is certainly good reason to exercise caution. Billy

Graham was famous for never walking into a hotel room until one of his staff entered it first, in case someone who didn't like him had set up a woman in a compromising stance with a photographer on hand. And many pastors and Christian leaders will not meet behind closed doors, or ride in a car alone, with a person of the opposite sex. There are situations that do require a certain amount of care and restriction, because of the dangers. Joseph, in the Bible, physically ran from temptation with Potiphar's wife (Genesis 39:12).

Having said that, however, women and men can be good friends with each other. They bring a perspective and a way of being to each other that can't really be replaced. The feminine and masculine viewpoints help balance us, grow us, and make us better people. Jesus himself had a deep and abiding friendship with two sisters, Mary and Martha, which also showed how he valued women in an age when women were seen as inferior (Luke 10:38–42).

Think about your family of origin. It was designed ideally so that you would be raised by a mom and a dad. Both contributed to your development and preparation for life. Does it make sense, once you have grown up and left home, to forever relate to the opposite sex in a meaningful way only if you are dating or married to the person? That limits a great deal of growth and friendship potential.

So evaluate your situation carefully. I have seen many solid marriages enhanced by opposite-sex friendships. The husband's female friend tells him he is entirely too left-brained and is not listening to his wife. She is an advocate and a guide for his wife and the marriage. The wife's male friend tells her that she doesn't let him have his "cave time" when he needs to be alone for a few minutes after work to recover from the day and transition into the family. He is an advocate for the husband and the marriage as well.

I recommend that both spouses spend time with the friend, so that the other spouse will feel more secure and know that he is safe, loved, and that everything is on the up and up. But the spouse who is feeling insecure needs to be heard and understood, because he or she comes first.

If, however, there is an ongoing character problem with opposite-sex relationships, things have to be different. For example, if a man tends to be flirty or sexually inappropriate with women as his norm, or he has been unfaithful, he needs to get counseling and help for those issues before taking a risk with a close female friendship. For the time being, he may need to be sober and stick with his male friends, not unlike how an alcoholic should avoid getting a job as a bartender.

The tricky question here has to do with the problem of a spouse who doesn't want her partner to have opposite-sex friends, but the issue is her fear and insecurity, not his character or love. In that situation, the risk is that he may curtail healthy, godly, and marriage-supporting connections so that she will not feel anxious, and then she never has to face and deal with her own fears and difficulties.

In that sort of situation, the one with the problem never deals with it, and the one without the problem pays for his spouse's injury. One option in this case is that the wife gets help for the problem, and the husband remains sensitive to her feelings, supporting her growth, and being totally trustworthy. I worked with a couple in which the wife found herself intensely jealous of any attractive woman her husband talked to, from a neighbor to work colleagues. Yet he was insanely in love with his wife. The root of the issue was that she had grown up with a distant father who had cheated on her mom, and that nightmare bruised her ability to trust a man's character. Once she realized the issue, she revisited her past, grieved the losses she experienced because of her dad, and was able to feel secure in her husband's love, resolving the dilemma.

BANISH SUPERIORITY

Finally, remember that "best" is not a morally superior category. Your best friend is your best friend because you and she are a great fit for each other, not because she is better than the rest of your friends. When you ask the waiter at the restaurant what he recommends, he may say, "My favorite is the steak or the pasta." Favorite is just favorite; it isn't superior. You and your BFs would not fit every other friendship scenario, so there is no better or worse here.

Remember the pain of junior high, when the cliques were in full bloom? There was a stinging moral tone to not being included. Stay away from that tone and be glad you're finding some great fits for yourself.

A Great Life Requires Great Friends

I have a friend who was struggling with a fragile marriage. Though she and her husband had been married many years, there was deep alienation between them. She was lonely and unhappy in the relationship and was considering ending it.

She had invested most of her life in her family and her job. The friendships she did have were more social relationships and neighbors; good people, but no one she really confided in about what was going on. This made the loneliness worse. She had never really known how isolated she was until her marriage began to go sideways, which became the tipping point that helped push her into finding some safe people to open up to.

When she formed these relationships, more from desperation than from anything else, she was surprised at their impact on her marriage. She wanted help for herself, but found that the marriage was helped as well. These people listened. They were empathic. They heard her experience at a deep level. But at the same time they didn't go the easy route and bash her husband, who was not present to defend himself. Instead, they encouraged her to grow, develop, change herself, while at the same time drawing clear boundaries with his behavior as well. Over time, she and her husband began moving toward one another again. This woman attributes a large amount of the marital growth to the impact of these "real" friends. Their support, unconditional acceptance, wisdom, and feedback were indispensable for her.

This is one of the many positive aspects of having best friends. They can make you a better person, enrich your life, and help heal other relationships in your life. We just have to recognize their potential value and importance.

2

The Accidental
Necessity

Best friendships can go on a long time without yielding their potential and value, unless we put focus and energy into them. The less focus and energy you exert, the less good you will receive. You can be proactive and take initiative to be intentional about improving your friendships. Or you can be passive and go with the flow and let things happen. If you're a nice person, you'll probably have friends either way. But being passive will not get you the great connections that being proactive will.

Let me illustrate: As a family, we have two old Labrador retrievers—Heidi and Casey. They've had a good long run, and we are very connected to them. In these later years of their lives, they have less energy and make fewer demands to play. It's easy to be a little passive with them: say hi when you get home, pat them on the head now and then, and make sure they are fed. And we have done that, especially when we've been busy with work or family activities.

When that's all we do, Heidi and Casey slow down even more. They will sleep all the time, become lazy, and I will even see an increase in health problems. We're not being negligent or unkind to them. We are just being lazy ourselves. But when we make sure we're playing with them every day, walking them, and taking them on excursions, I can see a shift. When we are being proactive, the dogs have more energy, are more alert, and act younger than they are.

Friendships are the same way. You probably are kind and warm with your friends, but you can neglect the care and maintenance of the relationship either in quantity (not enough time) or quality (what you do with the time). You may not notice it immediately, but friendships will either improve or diminish, depending on how proactive you are. Take initiative, and you will reap the rewards.

A Chance Encounter

A BF relationship can begin in any number of ways, most of them accidentally as you are going through life. Your closest friendships probably didn't begin with an interview and a questionnaire, though the online age is changing all this.

While you can post "friend wanted" ads on Craigslist, and people can request to be your "friend" on Facebook, most best friendships begin as we simply pass through life and meet someone we like.

In researching this book, I asked people about how they met their closest friendships. Most of the sources were the following:

- Your kids are friends with their kids
- Childhood and school days
- College
- Workplace
- Neighborhood
- Church
- Introduction from a mutual friend
- Chance encounter

One friend of mine said, "Ten years ago, I was talking to a neighbor and we got into how we need to walk in the mornings. We just started doing that. It was about the walking, and having someone to do it with was just a way to make the time more pleasant. But now—and I didn't expect this—the friendship is the main thing, and the walking is secondary. She and I have become very close."

Wherever you met your BF, you were what is called "relationship-seeking." That doesn't mean you were on the hunt or desperate. It simply means that within you, there was an openness to good, new relationships. We are scouting even when we don't think we are.

When I walk our dogs in the neighborhood, they pull on their leashes like crazy and want to play when they see another dog. If they see another person, however, they don't respond and just continue on their way with me. As I understand it, their strong reactions to other dogs are responses to memories of one another and of their litter days. They are affected by those like them.

In the same way, we are watching, listening, and aware of those around us. We may have a full and good life, but still respond to the other "dogs on a walk" if they seem warm and interesting.

The point is that most of us are always looking for more good relationships, but we really haven't figured out the specific qualities we are looking for, nor do we really know the path to accomplish that. The beginning of a BF relationship may be quite random. But its care and maintenance should not be, if you want to get the most out of it.

Often, however, we don't even get to address or experience those qualities because other factors come into play. I believe that for most people, your BFs, while being a great source of support, are being significantly underutilized. Your friendship simply isn't providing close to what it could for either of you. The potential is not being released. The good news is that, with a little exploration and effort, you can reverse the underutilization and actually maximize what can be there for both of you, if you are up for it.

LACK OF AWARENESS

One reason for underutilization is that many individuals simply aren't aware of the potential and the place of BFs in life. They have them, care about them, and appreciate them, but not for the value they could bring to life.

In these situations, best friends are more like what I would call "companions." That is, they are people you are close to, but the purpose of the relationship is more about going through life with someone, floating down the river in a connected state. There is a true closeness here and a lot of good exists in that attachment. But what is missing is that companions don't really impact our lives; they are on the periphery of it. They may be a sounding board and someone to talk with about what's going on at home and at work, but there is no real "ask" or "give" involved. They are not central to the decisions and choices we make in life. They are great for backyard barbecues or soccer games with the kids, and they are encouraging people, but it tends to end there.

Often, when we don't know the real value of a BF, we will outsource issues to other people that the BF could handle. Some people will seek out a pastor or a therapist when there is a life struggle, and tell their BF about it much later. "I didn't want to burden you," or "I was embarrassed," or "I don't want to be a high-maintenance person" are common excuses.

As a psychologist, I have seen that a good BF can bring struggles to light. Before a problem becomes a clinical issue and requires professional attention, good friends can do a world of good in preventing smaller things from becoming big things.

You will also notice that when BFs don't have their proper place, they are treated as expendable. Marriage, kids, dating, and work concerns are primary, and friendships seem to have to fit around all that. Think about how often you reschedule a coffee or lunch with a friend when other matters take over. We rarely move mountains to keep our BF times sacred.

Certainly family matters come first. But if you notice a pattern of shifting your friendships so that they are always at the bottom of the list, see this as a problem in recognizing value.

One thing that encourages me is that the current crop of young adults seems to place a high value on friendships. They are affiliation-driven and are invested in community at a deep level. An indicator of this is the emergence of terms such as *bromance* and *womance*, referring to deep and personal connections between same-sex friends. This generation is very "relationship-seeking," and not simply on a romantic level. We have a lot to learn from them.

If you are aware that you are not giving proper value to your BF relationships, I recommend that for the next ninety days, you put an asterisk beside your next calendared meeting with your BF, right next to his name. That will be a little signal to you that there needs to be a very good reason for bumping that meeting off. Unless it's a crisis, you and your BF will meet. It is a way to reorient yourself to the value that close friendships bring.

LOVE INTEREST AS THE ONLY BF

I sometimes hear, "My wife is my best friend; I don't need anyone else but God." In this scenario, the person's spouse or romantic love interest is the only source and center of the "real stuff" in life. The romantic connection, whether it is a dating relationship or a fifty-year marriage, is the only place the energy goes. Friendships are appreciated and seen as good things, but you don't "go there" with anyone but the person you love.

On one hand, you have to affirm the depth and commitment of someone with a great marriage. There are few things more wonderful than that sacred and lifelong attachment. A marriage must be protected and nurtured, which takes time, vulnerability, investment, good boundaries, and energy.

However, one of the best things you can do to make your marriage greater is for each of you to have best friends. This is not just a positive suggestion; it is a necessity for several reasons.

First, marriage requires other sources. Your spouse can't meet every relational need you have, nor can you meet his. We have lots of needs, and in varying amounts. Think about the list of friendship qualities that have been mentioned in this book. Can your spouse meet every one of those at every moment? Would it work for her to attempt to? Try showing a list of these to your spouse and asking, "Are you able to do all this for me, on a more-or-less weekly basis, for the rest of our lives?" If your spouse is healthy, she will freak out a little, and then say, "We need a small group."

We were not designed to have one person meet our deepest needs. We were designed for community. There is a great, healthy balance in a couple's life where their one-on-one times come first, but they are also going out and doing things on a frequent basis with others as well. Included in that are also "my friends" and "your friends." These other relationships need to be deep and real connections. If relationship is the fuel of life, these BFs fuel not only the person, but the marriage as well.

I was talking to a friend of mine about the impact his friends have on his marriage, as he has several very good BFs. He and his wife not only do "couple stuff" with other couples, but on a regular basis he also makes sure he has deeper and more connected conversations with a few men he is close to and trusts. He said, "I come back to my wife with more appreciation for her and more interest in her world." His wife agrees that she has experienced the benefit of his having close friends as well.

That is a good diagnostic for your BFs if you are married. If you come back after a night out with your friends, and you can't get past your spouse's faults and are noticing a few more because of what they are saying and observing about him, you may want to curtail those friendships. Good BFs tell the truth, but they also do everything they can to help your marriage grow and develop.

Also, think about all the conflicts that newly married

couples have about this. One of them has a group of close friends that he has spent the years of his life with. The other doesn't really gravitate toward close friends. When the marriage begins to move into its post-honeymoon phase, often the one without the friendship background will resist those relationships: "You want to be with them more than me." On the other hand, the friended spouse will begin to feel smothered and controlled: "You don't want us to get a life."

If the friended spouse is neglecting the marriage, that needs to stop and be redirected. But if not, the other spouse needs to look at what she is afraid of and resisting. She may be scared their connection cannot hold on in competition with his friends. But if there is a problem in the connection, cutting off his friends will not help that problem; it will create even more alienation and distance between the two. This spouse often needs to deal with her own insecurities about how lovable she is in the first place, and about her trust in the love and strength of the marital bond. When she works on that, she often sees that good friends will increase the connection she desires with her spouse.

This is a common problem with husbands, probably more than wives. Since most women have the relational edge on men, sometimes a husband will unknowingly put his wife in the position of being the only deep relationship he has, the only social conduit. She is the one he confides in, unloads his joys and fears to. She is the one who is safe for him to be vulnerable with.

This is a mixed blessing. Many women would give anything for a man who would connect at that level with his wife. It is always much better than disconnection and empty space. But the problem comes when the wife has to take on too much: his emotions, his reflections of life, his opinions, and his dreams. Over time, this can morph from a marriage connection to a child-parent connection, for that is what parents do with their kids. And, if they are honest, the "parent" spouse will admit that it is a lot to bear, and that they would like it if their spouse had other sources who could also listen to and support him. You don't dump the entire truckload of hay on one horse!

A LACK OF VULNERABILITY

Life is too short to go through it without vulnerability. We all need to be transparent about our inner selves, needs, mistakes, and emotions with someone. Best friends are the best place for that need.

Actually, we really don't have to be vulnerable. We can pretty much survive and have a decent life of sorts with no one knowing us at a deeper level. We will suffocate without air and starve without food. But if we never let anyone in on how we really feel or what we need, we can still grow up, find a career, get married, raise a family, have barbecues, and go to church. The effects of a lack of vulnerability are subtle and long term, so it is common for some people to simply live lives absent of transparency. Eventually, though, quality-of-life problems, intimacy conflicts, and emotional issues can arise.

Lack of vulnerability can happen for a number of reasons: past trust violations, relational hurts, or simply a lack of exposure to authentic connections. Whatever the cause, it reduces our need and hunger for best friends. It takes some amount of effort to have friends, but it takes risk and trust to establish the vulnerability we need to have best friends. So some people simply have never made themselves vulnerable and are a little relieved they have not.

If you struggle with a lack of vulnerability, you need to face it and open up. If you admit an insecurity, a need, or a past hurt to a good person, you will be amazed at how much good, and how much value, you will experience from a best friend. If you have a hard time opening up to your friend, talk to him about that. Tell him, "I am really uncomfortable talking about what's really going on." That will often break the ice for both of you. But if that is also too scary, talk to a therapist about it and work it out. Directly or indirectly, you must face your fears of being vulnerable with those who matter most.

Become intentional in your present and future friendships. It will not require overhauling your life, but it will pay off in great rewards.

3

Life Is Better When
We Are Hanging Out Together

One of the greatest perks in my life is the "no-purpose phone call." It is when one of my friends calls during the day for a few minutes, just to ask what's going on. No agenda, no project, no pitch. I try to do a few of these every week as well. The no-purpose phone call often gives me a boost, not unlike an afternoon coffee. It is amazing the good that happens when you talk to someone you truly and simply like.

This first element is where it all begins in great friendships. You attach or bond. There is a mutual affection between you. Attachment is why people call, meet, text, and go on vacations together. Life is better lived around that person than without him.

LIKING

Attachment actually has two parts in friendship—liking and connecting. Liking has to do with being drawn to a person, and it can be for any number of reasons: her personality, warmth, interests, or sense of humor, for example. Liking is necessary to being a best friend. If you don't like someone, it is difficult to spend the time and energy needed to build the relationship. Think about it. What if you had to say, "I know this person is good for me, but I am really uncomfortable around him, and he is a drain on me"? Or "I should spend time with her. I know she is good for me, but we just don't have any chemistry"? It would be like going to physical therapy to get your sprained ankle healthy. Good for you, but not pleasant at all. That simply doesn't work in best friendships.

Some people say liking is just a matter of personal chemistry, and you can't control that—it is what it is. But I don't believe that's true. Liking can change, and I have seen it happen often. As we grow and change, our tastes and preferences change along with us. We hate coffee at ten years old, but love it at twenty-five. We love fast cars, but then start looking for something with a smoother ride.

In relationships, preferences often change because we have been deepened and transformed in some way. Our capacity to see good things in those people, and to be drawn to that, moved us past a stylistic or distancing mechanism.

I was once in a small group in which I was friends with two guys who didn't really like each other. It was a little awkward when the three of us were together. I got along with both, but the connection stopped there. One man's style was more buttoned-down and conservative; the other's was looser and more liberal. Both were good people, but they were different and rubbed each other the wrong way. The first guy felt that the second was often provocative and childish, while the second one saw the first as parental and judgmental. From time to time, they would get into it, and I wondered if they would ever like each other.

They, however, continued being involved in the small group, and continued to make attempts to be as vulnerable and transparent as possible with each other. Over time, as they kept up the process, they began to feel affection for one another. They understood each other at deeper levels. The structured one began to feel appreciation for the spontaneity of the looser one and also knew where that came from in his past. The second man, in turn, was drawn to the strength of the first one and knew from his past why he had to be the strong one. They dug beneath the styles to the core person, and they felt compassion and began to truly like each other.

So if you find yourself in a shared situation with someone whom you'd like to like but can't, don't assume it will always be that way. Be vulnerable yourself as you get to know the person's story. Dig into what turns you off or triggers you about them. You can often see many improvements in how you feel about the person and who they are.

Keep in mind, though, that even if you begin to like someone, not everyone you like can be a best friend. What's more, even if you like someone right away, know that being drawn to them is no guarantee that the person is good for you, or that the relationship is the right one either. Sometimes we are drawn to a certain type of person because of some not-so-healthy reasons. People often pick people out of their emptiness or brokenness, not because this is the right person to get close to. The rescuer, for example, finds an addict to fix, often so that she can fix herself. The people pleaser is drawn to an overly assertive individual so that he will not have to speak up and be direct and honest. The introvert picks an extrovert so that she won't have to figure out how to reach out and take relational risks.

We hear that opposites attract, especially in romantic relationships; however, it is often not true, and isn't a good guide for picking the right people. Pick people based on principles and avoid the crazy "I found my missing piece" idea.

These attractions will never pay off over time. That is why you need to be aware of what drives you toward certain people, and to be brutally honest with yourself. Otherwise, the risk is great that after the initial attraction, the friendship will turn out to be an unbalanced and unhealthy one.

CONNECTING

The other piece to attachment in friendship is connection, which goes deeper than liking. Connection provides a transfer of grace between two friends. Just like cars need gasoline, we need grace in our friendships to sustain ourselves and our relationships as well. God designed us with a need for people that can be met at the deepest level by our best friends. When our BFs are not there, we are uncomfortable and know something is wrong. Paul described similar feelings for his friends: "We are not withholding our affection from you, but you are withholding yours from us" (2 Corinthians 6:12).

You have probably had the experience of driving away from a coffee or lunch with someone and asking yourself, "Was anyone home?" There were two talking heads, but no real connection. Hopefully, you have also had the alternative memory of feeling less alone, more full inside, and even more connected to yourself after a shared meal with someone. When people talk about their feelings, struggles, and each other, things connect.

Recently, I was under a lot of pressure with deadlines on several projects and was feeling quite overwhelmed. I had a lunch appointment with a BF that I almost cancelled because I didn't think I had the time. But afterward, I was more at peace and energized to organize and execute my tasks. The connection helped me move along.

Connection comes from being open and vulnerable, and allowing yourself to feel a need for the other person. When you are under stress and feel alone or overwhelmed, you look for contact with your BF to be present with you. Connection is what creates a BF in the first place.[1] It opens the door to moving into more vulnerable areas of need, struggle, and failure, where it is most difficult to be honest, yet the most important.

DEEPENING THE ATTACHMENT

To deepen the attachment of the relationship, it's important to act in ways that foster trust and openness to each other. Attachment among best friends works best when both people are vulnerable and open, and make that vulnerability a normal part of the friendship. This is important because without mutual vulnerability, one person becomes the counselor and the other the counselee, which is not the true nature of friendship. Friendship is always a two-way street.

Build vulnerability into your friendship. Take the lead in bringing your needs for grace, validation, acceptance, understanding, and safety to the relationship. Put your cards on the table, face up. While we all need to talk about daily life, kids, politics, and so forth, go deeper. Talk about how you feel, not just how you think. Bring up what concerns you, frustrates you, or saddens you in your life.

Here are a few questions that will give both of you some hooks to hang your thoughts on in your quest for a deeper attachment. Give yourselves time to ramble and be spontaneous. Often, things will pop up that will bring you closer together, and these conversations will be times of connecting the dots for both of you.

- *What brought us together in the first place?* The history helps to provide perspective, whether it was a sports event, or a neighborhood meeting, or a church function. This is the random occurrence that most friendships begin with.

- *Why do you think we like each other? What is it that brings us together?* This puts the "like factor" under the glass a bit. You may find that you like each other's easygoing nature, values, or cynical view on life. Recognize and affirm those as good and valuable.

- *How are we doing on making a personal connection with each other? Do we feel safe talking about what's going on in life? Are we making it safe for the other person as well? Is our relationship a good place to go deeper, because there aren't a lot of places in life to do that?* This is a bigger step. Some friends will jump in and want to talk about this, because they feel the need and aren't afraid. Others will be more tentative. Take people at their level. Just the fact that you broached the subject is going to help over time.

- *What can we do to make the relationship a better place to connect?* Now you are open to suggestions from each other, which can improve things. Matters may come up, such as:

  - ❖ I'd like to spend more of our time on deeper matters and less on the activities of life.
  - ❖ Sometimes I feel you're uncomfortable with my emotional responses, and I'd like to know if that's true and what it's about.
  - ❖ I think sometimes I keep some distance with you because you seem to have it together, and I know I

don't. I guess I need to know you don't think I'm a total loser when I talk about problems.

That is the pattern. It's simple, and you may find that you have begun with one of these, and an entire discussion occurred. Go with where the interest and energy are. Unless you have a tough timeline to follow because of scheduling difficulties, less structure and more depth will get you where you want to go. How would you feel if you were opening up to your BF and she said, "That's great, now on to the next part"? You probably would stay shut down after that.

This is how BFs stay attached and improve the attachment. It is worth the initial discomfort in the returns you will both experience. Remember the no-purpose phone calls I mentioned earlier? Even if you don't have a lot of time, use the call to go deeper. Take the initiative to go beyond how work and family activities are going. You can say, "I was thinking about the situation in your marriage. How's it going?" Or "I wanted you to know that I really appreciated how you let me ramble and talk forever about my crazy mother." Each of these conversations paves the way for a better and more complete friendship. It's worth it.

4

The Time
Investment

My assistant gave me our worksheet for the day. I ran down the questions and projects we were working on, and I looked at the fourth item: "Dinner with Tom: look at available dates." On the surface, it looks like just another social event to schedule. But it reflected something much more important. Tom is one of my best friends, and he and I meet regularly for dinner. In fact, I see him more than I do a lot of my geographically closer friends. Here is the significant part: Tom lives in another state.

This works because while Tom and his family reside elsewhere, he travels regularly to my area of the country for his job. But it really works because Tom makes it work. He calls and makes sure I am finding an available time when he is in town. He is relentless and does not feel rejected when I don't always do the same. He is a great example of how BFs should make sure that they stay connected. Tom is a better man than I am in this regard, but I am improving in this area because of his modeling.

Here is the point: best friendships require time to grow and produce the great relationships we need. There simply is no substitute for time. We need both quality and quantity, and can use time as an advantage in our friendships.

INVEST EARLY

When a relationship is in the early stages, say this is a friend who is becoming a best friend, we need more frequency. The earlier the friendship, the more frequency is required. It is difficult to create a BF when the beginning lunches, coffees, dinners, or outings are few and far between. That is not enough time to build the foundation. The psychological term for this is *internalization*, which refers to the process of taking in experiences you have with other people. This is more than memory, such as how we remember the ingredients of a recipe. Internalization includes the cognitive, but goes beyond that to the relational and the personal. It adds up and grows over time. We remember a vacation. We internalize the person we went on vacation with. The people we connect with on the deepest level become emotional realities within us, and we keep them inside us. Children develop a sense of being loved and secure when they have "internalized" parents who were consistently warm and loving. They have an emotional image, or picture, inside that cheers them on, encourages them and comforts them in times of stress.

Next to our parents, siblings, family of origin, our spouse, and our kids, BFs are the people we internalize the most. The encounters build up and accumulate inside us over time, in the same way that an investment account builds up every time we make a deposit into it. We deposit a vulnerable conversation, or a sorrow that we share. And that friend becomes more and more significant and meaningful to us.

Think about your current BFs. You probably will see that the beginning stages involved more frequency. That is partially because of a honeymoon effect where she's a new person who is interesting to you and vice versa. But this beginning period also is the way God designed you, so that your relationship has a foundation, that you are "rooted and established in love" (Ephesians 3:17).

Once you both have invested in the friendship, your BF will be part of your life—most likely for the rest of your life—even if you don't see each other as often as you'd like. He is a consistent and stable part of yourself. You can't really "forget" a best friend the way you can a friend. They are just too deeply ingrained in your personal fabric. That is why you can talk to a BF you haven't seen for years and immediately be connected at a deep and satisfying level. The old experiences are working for you.

If you didn't have your shared experiences, you wouldn't have the relationship you presently experience. That isn't to say that a new relationship can't go deep quickly. Certainly these happen. And they can often form a best friendship over time. But it doesn't make sense to label someone a BF without actually putting the time in. Easy in means easy out. You don't want it to be easy; you want something substantive over time. You need the relational equity as a foundation. Call it "a great new relationship" or "a really nice person." But don't call it a best friendship yet. My advice is to wait a year before you label him a BF. I say this not because it is a bad label; it's a great one. But it hasn't been earned yet. You need to go through seasons of life with that person: good times, hardship, anniversaries, holidays, stress, family experiences, and differences. Look at the term "best friend" as an earned degree, not an honorary one. But once you two have earned the status, the equity will be there for you, and you do not have to spend the time that you did in the beginning (although if you can, by all means, do).

More Is Better

In the end, with significant relationships, more is simply better. If you can meet more often and still pull off a balanced life, that is a good thing. Why not? There is a lot of good there for you: more safety, acceptance, vulnerability, and honesty. These are not aspects of life that we can have too much of. It is impossible to have too much of a great relationship. It may be impossible to have all the time you need for it. But if you have the time, take it. Don't be disheartened or give up quickly if it's hard logistically to stay in touch. Take initiative, like my friend Tom does, to meet with your BFs frequently. Unless there is a dependency issue, two people who are very good friends can't help but make each other's life better.

Research is now showing that who you spend time with influences your behavior even more than your BFs. Scientists are using the tracking abilities of smartphones to look at the patterns of our behavior, and are finding that our habits and tastes are more highly marked by the people around us who may be simply acquaintances, than those BFs we don't spend much time with.[1] To put it another way: proximity matters. Therefore, as much as possible, it makes sense to spend more time with those you are closest to.

The best and highest example of this, of course, is a healthy marriage. When two people share their lives, they are together an enormous amount of time, in frequency and in duration. And in a good marriage, more is better. Certainly each spouse needs their own space and friends of their own. But ultimately, marriage was designed so that more time together means more closeness, growth, depth, and joy. My wife's father died after forty-six years of marriage to her mom. One of the things her mother said during the funeral reception was "It wasn't long enough." That is not only a statement for a great marriage, but for a great friendship. We don't always think that way. But consider who, today, would say that about you if you passed away suddenly, besides your family. You need some BFs who think that of you as well.

THE RIGHT AMOUNT

How do you know if you're not spending enough time with your BF? Is there a minimum? It depends. Some BFs would love to spend more time together, but either circumstances or a disconnection between them prevents it. I think the best way to determine the right amount is by what happens because of the relationship, what is the fruit of the connection. If the right things are happening, you're at least hitting the minimum. If they aren't, it may be that more time is needed. Below are the basics of the encounter as I see them.

1. *Caught up.* You spend enough time with each other that you are caught up on the essential events of your lives: family, relationships, job, health, and so forth. That takes a certain amount of time to do. Not a great deal, but some. Are there large informational gaps between you and your BF? Or, if you were asked what's going on with that person, could you summarize her current life's important events? While some details can be shared through social media, make sure you're connecting face-to-face to get the depth. Sometimes people will say, "We're above all the mundane trivia. We connect at a soul level; we don't need those externals." I believe in connecting at a soul level too, but that soul has a body! That body has a history and went through experiences that formed what that soul is today: events, relationships, accomplishments, failures, and losses. I would never coach or counsel someone without having some idea of his life context. You both need enough time to be caught up.

2. *Connected.* Whatever it takes to stay emotionally connected, that is your frequency minimum. Caught up and connected are not the same thing. One is about significant life events, and the other is about intimacy. Ultimately,

connection is the core of why people become BFs with each other. They bring closeness to each other. They are less isolated, less alone, and more loved inside. If you both feel you are attached, even when you aren't together, you're probably OK. If you find that it's hard to feel close or attached to the person when you are away, look at that as a problem to be solved. More to the point, if you find that it's difficult to open up with the person when you are together, yet there is no relational conflict between you, and you don't have a psychological problem in making attachments, it's probably time to increase the frequency.

3. *Honest.* Truth is something BFs value and prize with each other. It is feedback and perspective that comes from a rich source of time and experience. It can be trusted. Honesty, however, takes time—probably more time than catching up and connection—and can be difficult to say and to hear. You need a time runway to be comfortable enough to be honest, especially on a deeper level. Think of it this way: if you only saw your closest friend for one lunch a year, how confrontational would you be? Unless he was getting ready to commit a felony, probably not very much at all. You would want to spend that precious time connecting and "being there" with the person. And that would be the right thing to do. What if you have a lunch twice a month for a

year? You would probably be more up front about things that concern you, and that would be a good use of the time you have. If you two never "truthed" anything at all in those twenty-six lunches, there was probably some fear in at least one of you. In other words, are you meeting and talking enough to get to some truth that might be important?

Think of these three things in your most important relationships. You may need to adjust the frequency in one or more friendships to keep them at the level you need them to be. If there is just not enough time to do that, while she can still be a BF and hold a special role with you forever, she may not be the kind of BF you have an ongoing, life-sustaining relationship with anymore. The friendship may be good for those times you can meet, or for a life crisis in which you know she will be there for you. That's not a bad thing, but it is a difference. Keep the two types of BFs in mind as you make your choices on what you do with your relationship time.

And if you find yourself not caught up, connected, or honest with those BFs who are currently in your life, it may be good to have some sort of a regular structure that you can both depend on: a breakfast, lunch, coffee, that sort of thing. It is one less thing to worry about to know that you have a regular time on your calendar. Or at least, by the end of the meeting, pulling out your calendars and planning the next time. I have had an ongoing lunch with a close friend for the past ten years. We have counted on that time as something we can both bring ourselves to and depend on, and it has been an important space for both of us. Structure exists to preserve connection. Use it if it helps.

There is a "sweet spot" of how much time to invest in your BF. My guess is that most of us could use a little more, with those people who matter the most. Make the investment.

5

BFs in a
Facebook World

Last week I asked my son Benny and his friend Lili, who are both students, what they thought of Facebook. Lili answered, "I like it and I don't like it." Surprised, because I don't know many people that age who are negative at all about Facebook, I asked her what she meant. She said, "I like it when I can connect with people I'm not around. But I also find that I get lazy and facebook people when I should be seeing or talking to them. That doesn't seem right." Her insightful response leads to the question: Does Facebook make friendships better, worse, or neither?

Most of the people I know are now using digital connections, from texting to email to social media such as Facebook and Twitter. We are connecting with others instantly and forming communities. Digital connections are also showing us how important people are to us, and how we constantly seek some sort of contact. This connection, especially social media, has an increased presence in our best friendships.

Not Real Life

While social media can be useful to maintain connections and increase acquaintances you may have in common areas of interest, most people do not meet their best friends through social media. There are exceptions, of course, such as high school classmates restarting friendships on Facebook, but for the most part, people simply meet their BFs face-to-face in some arena of life and then use social media to stay connected with those individuals. There are simply too many obstacles in starting up a close friendship over social media, such as the time involved, not being able to know who the person really is, and understanding the life context of another person.

Once you have an established friendship, digital connection, especially social media, is essentially neutral. It is not good or bad in its essential nature; rather, it is a magnifying glass. In BF relationships, social media makes good things better and bad things worse.

When people have a healthy and honest friendship,

Facebook is a great way to stay in touch because it is so convenient and efficient. If you have five minutes between meetings, you can post a comment on a friend's wall and read something she has written about the kids or a trip she is on. I personally get a great deal of satisfaction out of communicating instantly with people I know around the world. It solves many of the problems of not being able to see or talk to someone you are close to. It does not tend to be all that substantive and personal, but it's a good connection on a social level.

The other side is true as well. If a relationship is struggling, it is hard to fix it over digital connections. Anything negative or confrontational seems much worse when you read it. In fact, I tell people to simply not confront each other digitally at all, as it is so easy for the responder to feel attacked or judged. Also, this sort of medium allows us to hide. We can present aspects of ourselves that are not true, or conceal parts that we don't want others to know about. It is a simple matter to construct a persona that is not really true. Suppose, for example, that you are struggling in a relationship, but don't want to be a downer for your BF. Then you'll tend to post pictures and chatty information, without getting to the heart of the matter. If you will be talking to her soon, that is one thing. You are simply waiting for an opportune conversation. But if you are avoiding the negative information, you are not helping your relationship develop. That doesn't mean you should convey it online. It means be intentional and find a time to be personal and present when you do.

INSTANTANEOUS DEPENDENCY

Another negative aspect of social media that affects friendships is the problem of not taking the time and effort to reflect and think of your own experience. We all need to have space to think our thoughts and feel our feelings. That is how identity is formed and is maintained. We need to know what we think and feel about anything from a movie we just saw, to a stress we just underwent at work, to a family struggle with a sick child, to what we learned from a Bible verse. When he taught Timothy how to live, the apostle Paul also told him to "Reflect on what I am saying, for the Lord will give you insight into all this" (2 Timothy 2:7). David told the Lord he would "meditate on your precepts and consider your ways" (Psalm 119:15). Reflection, meditation, and thought require a certain amount of being separate from others so that we know where we are. It doesn't mean that our opinion is final. It is simply where we have landed so far, and now we can use our relationships to clarify reality for us, and bring a new and better perspective into play, which benefits us.

When people are not able to do this, they go to others to receive reality, not to clarify it. In the psychological world, this is called a dependency issue. They depend on others' external views and are afraid to trust their internal ones. Children go to parents and ask them, "Which friends should I invite to the party?" Their dependency requires that they get information from Mom and Dad, which is internalized over time, and then eventually, they will make their own decisions. But some adults go to their friends and, before they have really thought and deliberated for themselves, will ask "Should I date this guy?" "What job should I take?" or "Should I move?"

The reason digital connection poses a problem here is because of its convenience, and because others are so willing to help and give perspective, not knowing that this might be a bad idea. You can just ask the questions you haven't processed for yourself, and get lots of information from your friends. I coached a female executive who was dating several men. As soon as she had a significant conversation with one of the guys, such as more vulnerability, or some conflict, she immediately texted, emailed, or facebooked her friends to see what they thought about what he said and what had happened. The result was that instead of coming to deliberate conclusions about these men herself, she was going with whomever she was getting the advice from at the time, and the advice was often contradictory. Finally, I asked her to wait awhile, think, and draw some conclusions about the guys before she went to her friends. This worked much better for her. Her information gathering was much more about getting feedback than about taking on someone's opinion. It's important to recognize how we are using social media and to course-correct when we need to.

KEEPING IT REAL

Some BFs are local and easy to meet with face-to-face; others are not. Email and social media are helpful with the latter. But face-to-face has not yet been matched, even with Skype. It is simply a matter of information. Being physically in the same space with someone else gives you access to words, tone, eye contact, body language, and many other ways of communicating. If you have moved recently from an area in which you were deeply connected, it's not a good idea to avoid finding local BFs while staying in touch with the old relationships via social media and email. You need the personal nature of face-to-face. While it's important to hold on to your BFFs, make sure you're connecting with new friends in person.

6

Speed Dial

My wife is very connected to Nancy, one of her dearest friends. I can almost predict that when something significant happens in Barbi's day, she will text either me or Nancy about it, depending on who she thinks is available. I came home from work one day and she told me that she had received an award as a teacher. I congratulated her and asked when she told Nancy. She answered, "Earlier today."

Best friends are the first place your brain should land when something important happens. We were not designed to go through landmark events and difficult times alone, mulling things over in our heads. Certainly we are always to think through things and pray about them. But when something impacts us, we should automatically think, "I need to tell my BF about this." This is because reality is more real to us when it happens in relationship. The highs and lows of life matter more when someone else is aware of them and we discuss them together. Galatians 6:2 tells us that we are to "carry each other's burdens." They are meant to be shared. We need to take advantage of the reality that someone cares about and is committed to us. Keeping our BFs caught up on the celebrations, the crises, and the complaints is what makes relationships worthwhile.

CELEBRATIONS

When a second-grade girl goes to her dad carrying a picture and says, "Look, I drew this." She wants and needs him to say something about the picture, like "That's really a great horse," or "I like the colors," or "I'm proud of you." Her dad's validation has just made the drawing, and her own efforts, more real to her. Validation has to do with knowing that your own experience counts, and matters, to someone else. When we are validated, we become more of ourselves. No one creates her identity all alone. It must happen in relationship. And even in the adult world, we need that sort of validation.

Being with your BF is a little like having a scrapbook of your most cherished memories. After each encounter, you place another experience into your memory banks: a great laugh, a shared sorrow, a vigorous disagreement, a knotty problem discussed. And that scrapbook is then available to you in those times you most need it. When you call your friend up and say, "I just landed the Gonzales account!" your BF's response of happiness and affirmation takes that experience and places it in the pages of the scrapbook. Then, when you need to draw on it, for example, when you lose the next two accounts, it is there for you. The relationship ensures that you will remember that you do know what you are doing and keep plugging away.

CRISES

Not only does your BF play a large part in the celebrations, including having a child, going on a vacation, or moving to a new home, but also in the difficulties of life. When you are in the middle of bad news, speed dial your BF. It can be a financial disruption, a date gone wrong, a child having trouble, or bad news in the marriage. Our minds take time to grapple with tough decisions when we are in the middle of them, and sometimes we just need someone to be there, to be present. It gets us out of being in shock and helps us get on with making the right choices.

A friend once called me when his teenaged daughter had just been caught in a bad drug situation. He is a very capable person, and I knew that he knew how to handle it. But he was caught off guard by the news. Within a few minutes, however, we crafted a game plan for the next few steps. My friend could have done this alone. But it would have taken him more time and more presence of mind than he had right then. That is the reason BFs speed dial each other.

COMPLAINTS

BFs vent to each other as well. That is, there are situations that we can't change or do anything about, but we simply need someone to blow off steam about it. It feels better to complain about something that frustrates us, even if nothing will really happen as a result of the conversation. At least our BF gets it, and we aren't alone in the experience. This is what happens in good marriages, when the spouses come together at the end of the day and vent about whatever bugged them. It has nothing to do with fixing, changing, or giving advice. It is about not being alone in it. That is why, if you have the advice gene, you must restrict it with your BF, or at least ask for permission before handing it out. On the other hand, be aware that you don't want to be chronically complaining yourself. Some people have an emotional attachment to protest or complaining, and you don't want to ruin a BF by that either.

Some people worry that they are venting wrongly or even too much. That can happen and there are a few things you can do to deal with these questions. Start with asking your BF if you're too intense or get too angry. She may say, "No, this is so normal." Or she may say, "Yes, it's a little much for me." If you hear that from more than one person, it may be time for a therapist to help you with the emotions. Also, look at the fruit of the venting. If it helps you solve problems, be responsible, and carry your own load, it's probably okay. But if it increases your dependency, so that you can't do life without it, you may need to get some help.

The Sooner the Better

Immediacy helps your BF help you. Being "in the moment" helps you to engage each other emotionally and relationally, while the experience is still fresh. By the time it has become a settled memory, your BF's contribution will have less impact. While your mind is still wet cement about what has happened, your BF can be a part of making sense of the experience. You see the apostle Paul's desire to be face-to-face with his friends in a similar way: "I long to see you so that I may impart to you some spiritual gift to make you strong" (Romans 1:11).

Nothing is more empty than a BF finding out several weeks after the fact that his friend had a loss or major life change, and didn't tell him. A friend of mine who lives in another state lost his job. I called him just because I had been thinking about him, and he told me then. When I asked, "Why didn't you call me?" he said, "I didn't want to be high maintenance." We talked further about this, because what he didn't realize was that in not staying current with me, he was, by definition, becoming high maintenance. Now I would worry that something big would happen in his life and I wouldn't know until I called.

If, like my friend, you don't want to be a burden on your BF, then you need to rethink this. That's what BFs are about. The misconception is that sometimes we think that sharing our struggles will drain others. But sharing is just talking and asking for support. It is not asking for a loan, or some magic answer, or a deliverance. And with good BFs, the sharing of the burdens actually brings more connection, intimacy, and closeness. The burden itself relieves the drain, instead of increasing it.

Who's on your speed dial? Certainly those who need you: your kids, your spouse, your work. Add those you need as well. Use it. Life is more real when you have talked about it.

7

What Matters Most

Values matter in great friendships.

A good friend of mine had gone through a difficult business partner relationship and had been treated badly. In fact, the ex-partner embezzled a large sum of money from him. It was very expensive for him, but more important, his trust had been broken in the relationship as well.

When we talked about it, I was surprised by his response. He had a chance to get even financially, and he was taking steps to hurt the ex-partner by a series of strategic moves. The motive was simply revenge.

I asked him how this squared with his beliefs, and he said, "For what he did to me, it's justified." I pressed him on it, and he was evasive: "Fair is fair." I couldn't pin him down to a meaningful conversation. It was clear that his hurt and anger were running things. But then I noticed that it was more than that: it was a value he had inside himself. We had several conversations in this vein, and it was always the same result. I tried to empathize with the hurt and to help him move past anger to letting go. I talked to him about how this ultimately would not work for him and wasn't a healthy stance for him to take. I asked him to seek other opinions and even get counseling for the issue. But he would not listen to my perspective. It was beyond an emotional reaction. He genuinely placed a higher value in getting even than in moving on. I then began to notice this pattern in other relationships of his. He would hold onto things against people in unhealthy ways instead of forgiving and letting go when he needed to.

After that, though, the direction of our friendship changed somewhat. I really liked him, we had a lot in common, and I always enjoyed our friendship. But I couldn't get as close to him as I wanted to. I wondered if he would take revenge on me as well, if I disappointed him. Sadly, I distanced myself. I didn't see myself as a better person than him; rather, the deeper connection just wasn't possible. We are friends to this day and still spend time together. But we are no longer best friends. For me, similar values are far too important when it comes to a best friendship.

Why Values Matter

Value is not a very exciting word. It doesn't evoke deep feelings of passion, joy, or intimacy. It doesn't put us into a state of bliss. But neither does a concrete slab at the base of a home, yet we don't want to be without one of these. Values are simply foundational to life and relationships, and we need to think about them in a serious way. Our own values will help determine the direction of our life, toward joy or misery. And they will help determine the quality of our friendships as well.

Values are simply representations of what is most important to us—the things that matter most. Those things of lesser importance might be opinions or preferences, but they aren't values.

Core Values

Core values are those general truths that guide all areas of your life. A few core values are more helpful than a large number of them. If you have too many, you can get sidetracked in an obsessive search for which values are the relevant ones. Remember that God gave us ten commandments, then summarized them into two: love God and each other (Matthew 22:35–40). A few core values may include:

- *Love:* making relationships and connectedness a primary part of my life
- *Responsibility:* taking ownership of my life and path
- *Freedom:* making my own choices, and supporting others' free choices
- *Forgiveness:* receiving and giving it for life's imperfections

Core values are also core to your deepest friendships. Can you imagine investing your friendship hours in someone who has little value for freedom and wants to control your time? Or someone who doesn't really want a relationship? Or someone who takes no ownership of their life or their effect on you? Or someone who keeps an account of every time you have let them down and reminds you of it? Something would break down sooner or later, as in the example of my friend. His value for forgiveness was low, while for me it was nonnegotiable, and it came between us.

CONTEXT VALUES

Context values are different from core values. They are your set of beliefs about how to conduct some specific areas of your life. For example, you may establish a set of values for your finances, your family, your business, your politics, your career, your health, or your political views. We all need to think through what is important to us and what is less so.

Best friends, however, can have more differences in their context values than their core values. Differences in context values promote debate, thought, growth, and humility, while core values are the cement of the connection itself. I have had many challenging and vigorous discussions among my best friends about matters of context value, and those talks have helped me grow, solidify some beliefs, and change others. If you don't have some meaningful context value differences in your closest circles, you may want to think about that. You may be becoming stagnant. It might be time to see if your friends have just been playing nice, or if you actually have an ingrown system of relationships.

For example, my wife and I have good friends that are all over the map in how to school kids: public, private, Christian, and in the home. We did our own research and talked to many people when we were determining what we wanted to do with our boys. And we have had many productive talks with people who landed on different answers for themselves.

I also have gymrat friends who are in great shape with low body fat and strict diets, and I have friends who are much more casual about these matters and whose greatest passion is a perfect bacon cheeseburger. And I love dinner conversations with both my politically conservative and liberal friends.

While your core values should be nonnegotiable, you should have best friends who don't share all of your context values. It's good to have a variety of friends who can help shape you.

The God Value

If you are a Christian, I hope you have close friends who are not Christians. The "holy huddle" mentality, where we only open our lives to others of our faith, simply does not work. People feel judged and "less than" if we keep them at arm's length because of spiritual values. And there are many wonderful people who don't share the Christian faith, yet who are very warm and caring and who have great character. Each of you may benefit from your connection and find that you have much to offer the other.

At the same time, however, if you cannot share the deepest part of yourself with another—your spiritual core—that imposes some sort of a built-in limit to the level of your intimacy. This says nothing about one person being better or worse than another; it just speaks to the nature of how relationships work. For that reason, I think it helps to make sure you are deeply connected to Christians who are safe and who want to grow with you.

If you have not found close Christian friends at all, you may want to find out why. Some Christians have been wounded by other Christians, and then have been shy with those of the faith. They have experienced judgment and condemnation from Christians, and yet have found acceptance and warmth from non-Christians. If that is the case, you must find a church setting where there is love and acceptance, and at the same time where there is truth and honesty. You will need to heal from the past and take some risks. There are lots of people who share your Christian values and who are also looking for whole and healthy relationships.

A BF Values Assessment

Figuring out what your core values are may be new territory for you and your BFs. People sometimes live by values that they have not actually articulated for themselves. Asking questions like, "Do I seem to be living these core values out?" and "What do you think are your own?" may be a helpful structure for you both. We often recognize that we believe things when we see the values stated: "I would never want to make you feel guilty about not being able to be with me if you are too busy" is a statement of the value of freedom, for example.

If you and your BF find vast differences in your core values, you are probably having some sort of ongoing relational conflict right now. It will help to talk about your differences and work them out, if possible.

Also, bring up the context values in the areas mentioned above. Ask, "Where are you and I on these?" It will be especially helpful to see if both of you can stay connected to each other, even with significant differences in values.

I was talking to a friend recently about a political view. I differed with him on a position, and he said, "Well then we'll have to part ways." I asked, "Are you kidding? Over that?" I was surprised to think he was ready to end the friendship then and there. After I challenged him on it, he thought about it and backed down. But it was a good example of how easy it is to confuse our passion with our connectedness, and our core values with our context values, and why it's important to identify both.

Stay separate in your context values with your BFs. And stay deeply connected to each other's hearts in your core values. In times of difficulty, your values will be a guiding light on your paths. And in times of happiness, they will accelerate your growth process as well.

8

Permission to Speak the Truth

How truthful are your best friendships? Are they places where you are both free to be honest, or where you have to walk on eggshells? Think about your greatest growth experiences in life, for example, when you understood yourself at a deeper level, or had some insight about life, career, or relationships. How many of these were influenced by someone being honest with you? In my experience, the truthfulness of others is critical to growth.

We all have a need to be able to speak the truth. It's inside us and must come out and be expressed. We are simply made that way. The Bible affirms that when we speak the truth from our heart, we will dwell in God's sanctuary (Psalm 15:1–2).

While honesty is often a core value in a best friendship, it is also a habit and a practice in our everyday lives. Being truthful keeps our minds clear, helps us solve problems, and helps us establish our own identity, responsibilities, and power. We simply begin to deteriorate relationally, physically, emotionally, and spiritually when we can't be honest. As Proverbs 10:18 puts it: "He who conceals his hatred has lying lips, and whoever spreads slander is a fool." In the books Henry Cloud and I wrote about boundaries, the core aspect is that truthfulness is simply part of God's righteousness and an essential piece of every good relationship.[1] Honesty is critical to your success, life, and growth.

THE TWO TYPES OF TRUTHS

There are two kinds of honesty dynamics in best friendships. The first one is being truthful *about yourself.* This may be about a value or a preference: you are conservative or liberal or somewhere in between. You like certain sports. You prefer small gatherings to large crowds. These are just ways people get to know each other.

You may also tell your friend that you don't like your job or that you are unhappy in a relationship. That is another form of being truthful about yourself. You may say that you are not satisfied with the direction of your life, or that you are questioning God and his ways these days. Instead of trying to put a positive spin on everything out of your own anxiety, you will just be honest about yourself. This helps the other person to trust you and feel more comfortable that they are with someone who has edges and personal definition.

The second type of relational honesty is harder than the first: being truthful *about the other person.* It is harder because of the risk involved, but it is also extremely valuable. Close friendships require this type of honesty to help both of you be the best people you can be. Who else is going to tell you that you have spinach in your teeth? Or that the guy you are dating is a creep? Or that sometimes you come across self-absorbed? You need to know this sort of info. Its value can range from helpful to vital. Don't you want the safest people in your life to be the ones to deliver it, instead of finding it out from someone who is judgmental of you?

A member of my staff is my "media wardrobe judge." She has very good taste, much better than mine, and when I am setting up for conference speaking or a video shoot, she will not hesitate to say, "You look awful in that; don't wear it." I appreciate her honesty. How can that hurt my feelings when she is helping me look better?

GRACE BEFORE TRUTH

For most of us, honesty is not always easy in our best friendships. While attachment emphasizes closeness and intimacy, honesty can bring up fears of hurt feelings, conflict, and alienation. If you have been "truthed without grace" by someone, even if they were spot on about what they said about you, the result is usually feeling condemned or judged. So we avoid harshly truthful people, and we avoid the risk that we might be that with someone else.

But that doesn't have to be the case. Two people who genuinely care about each other can actually give and receive the truth, and still feel close and supportive of each other. It will take a little work, practice, and courage, but it is worth it.

Always remember that while grace and truth come together, grace comes before truth. Truthfulness requires building up relational equity in your friendship. It's hard to swallow the pill when you don't have enough time to feel that the person dispensing it is on your side. I think, however, that most BFs have ample amounts of equity. In my observation, most BFs are too careful with each other, and too afraid of hurting the other or rocking the boat. I think it is because we are not used to the "truthing" end of life and don't have a lot of experience where it helped and didn't harm a connection. Try taking advantage of all the positive and affirming experiences and words you have between each other. There is probably more goodwill there than you think.

Reflect on the ratio of grace to truth in your best friendships. Generally speaking, people who are stronger in attachment than they are in honesty will have more friendships than those who are the other way around. It's hard to warm up to a really honest person who is weak in connections, even though you know they are good for you.

Think about the TV show *American Idol.* Simon Cowell was one of the most significant factors in the show's amazing success. No sugarcoating. And he was the one who, sometimes even in a mean and cruel way, called it as he saw it. Even so, he isn't generally regarded as the first person you'd want to go to when you need someone to understand your inner world!

In comparison, the other judges have been criticized for being too easy—"You can do better, I know you can; just believe in yourself, find your center, and I want to see you back here"—with some people who in reality just had no business being there in the first place. Ellen DeGeneres reportedly quit because she was uncomfortable giving negative feedback and wanted to be more nurturing. Think about all the helpful though tough information these judges withheld, and that the contestants didn't get the advantage of. So with the *AI* extremes in mind, keep grace plus truth, but grace must dominate.

CONFRONTING THE RIGHT WAY

You will also sometimes encounter triggers and resistances in your friendships when truth comes up. Some people, because of past hurts or their own character issues, equate truth with condemnation and don't see any difference. So when you are positive, they feel connected. When you bring up something honest, they feel persecuted and attacked by you. There is no middle ground. If this is a minor issue, BFs can talk about it, deal with it, and get past it. It's basically solved by reassurance and openness. If it is major, and there is no way your BF can hear truth at any level from you, no matter how kind you are, you may want to evaluate if this is a true BF or not. There may simply be a limitation on the truthfulness the relationship can handle. On the other hand, if you have a good friendship with someone, they may surprise you with how well they handle the truth you offer them when it's wrapped in grace.

I was having lunch with a few friends to get caught up. Paul had, over the previous few months, dropped out of contact with the rest of us. He had gone somewhat off the grid. We hadn't seen him around, and it was hard for our schedules and his to come together.

During the lunch, Keith brought up Paul's absence and asked him what was going on. Paul's response was that his business had changed drastically with the economic downturn, and he had just been unavailable. Keith challenged that and said, "I get that, but you haven't even returned my phone calls."

Things got a little tense, and Paul replied, "Actually, if I have to admit it, you are right. I haven't returned your phone calls because you come on pretty strong, and I thought you would push me into meetings with you, when I don't have time. So I have avoided you."

That was when I stepped in and said, "Paul, you are right: Keith does come on strong sometimes. But you know Keith well, as we all do. You have known for years that he is for you and not against you. I would want you to take a look at why you don't feel OK about calling Keith and simply telling him, 'No, I'm buried at work, and I won't be available for awhile.'"

Keith said, "I do get pushy, and I'm sorry about that. But if you did tell me you are swamped, I would respect that. I just didn't know what was going on with you, when I couldn't reach you."

Paul's face turned thoughtful before he said, "You're right. I just got a little worried and didn't trust that you were really on my side. I won't do that again." For a few hours after the lunch, I was worried that Paul had been alienated by the conversation. I was relieved when I received an email from him that afternoon thanking us for our time and honesty and wanting to schedule another time to meet and catch up. But Paul is that kind of a man. He values friendship, he values truth, and he values the opportunity to grow.

Certainly this wasn't a normal businessman's lunch, and most of mine aren't like that. But we are very close friends, and it was a powerful and helpful encounter. In our way, Keith and I both pushed Paul to grow in the area of handling conflict. It was uncomfortable. But if comfort is the only value in a friendship, we may as well make friends with a leather recliner and be done with people. Best friends are completely honest with each other and push each other to grow.

One of the most meaningful things you can do with a best friend is to see the potential in her and be part of helping her reach it. You may notice a blind spot that is hampering her life. Or you may see that she doesn't see something awesome that she is capable of. Get in the mix and help her be a new person! That is what the New Testament teaches is one of the central reasons for us to be with each other and connect with each other: "From him the whole body, joined and held together by every supporting ligament, grows and builds itself up in love, as each part does its work" (Ephesians 4:16).

THE TWO TYPES OF GROWTH

When challenging BFs to become better people, it's important to know that growth has two distinct aspects to it. First is the "good to great," as business guru Jim Collins calls it.[2] Good to great refers to those capacities and potentials you have that aren't yet realized. An ability, a dream, a passion, or a possibility that has stayed at the "OK" level, but could go to the "fantastic" level. For example, an individual who is gifted in music, but hasn't really developed it. Or someone who has an idea for a web-based business, but hasn't put any structured effort into it. Or a person who connects deeply with people, and yet has not thought about putting that to use in some ministry context.

Think about a close friend right now, and I will bet that you see some specific potential in her that she does not. It is just part of the human condition. You may have even said, "Have you ever thought about writing a blog on that?" before the conversation quickly turned to something else.

Be more intentional about this. Don't let her redirect the topic with, "I'm really not that good. So how are the kids?" Push her to talk about her anxieties and insecurities a little. This doesn't mean be controlling or a pain, but let her know this is important. What if, a year from that conversation, she was published and being paid for writing? You'd get a lot of satisfaction from your contribution.

The other aspect of growth is "broken to good," referring to the healing process. We not only have unrealized potentials, we also have baggage, issues, hurts, and wounds. These can be emotional or relational scars from the past, where harmful experiences changed how we looked at life.

When someone has a brokenness, time alone will never heal it. Time does not, in and of itself, heal all things; although time plus relationship and truth can heal just about anything. But we have a tendency to ignore a hurt, or try to live around it or above it. It takes work, effort, and discomfort to heal trust issues, fears of intimacy, guilt messages, addictions, and the like.

That is where best friends come in. Be the agent of healing: let your friend know that you want him to have a better life, and you care enough to make it a topic of conversation. To tell a good friend, "I want you to see a therapist to get some help on this" is one of the most growth-producing things anyone can do. You can't do the healing yourself—only God, your friend, and the counselor can. But you can be the one who helps to make it something a person considers as a real and valid choice.

My wife and I were having dinner with a neighbor couple who we really connected with. But when the gals paired up in one part of the house for a few minutes, and the guys did the same, the husband mentioned some significant struggles they were having. I felt a great deal of compassion for both of them but knew a late-night conversation wouldn't fix the areas they were dealing with. So I encouraged him to get a marital therapist and suggested one I knew who would do a good job.

Two weeks later my neighbor told me they had made an appointment and felt some hope for the first time. My point is that all of us are dysfunctional at some level, and we all need help. Be the friend who goes beyond empathy, be honest, and help your friends get the healing they need.

The Skill of Pushing

Unless you are doing an intervention, be careful not to be extremely and bluntly direct with your friend in a crisis. But don't let something go that is important to growth for her either. When you want to push her, you have to be open yourself. Ask her to help you be the most highly achieving, healthiest person you can be. This will allow her to hear you as well, when it's her turn. Say, "One thing I want in life is to have a good life and reach whatever potential I have. Will you pinpoint areas that you see in me that I'm not growing in and need to?" You may find an immediate, "Wow, when you said that, I thought about your math abilities and how I think you have a lot of potential in that area."

Be prepared for avoidance and deflection. We tend to avoid matters that are tough and keep it comfortable. Instead, gently return to the hard matter. You might say, for example, "I know your child's school problems are hard to talk about. It's painful. But if you're OK with it, I'd like to press ahead with it. Maybe we can find a solution. At the least, you'll know you have a friend who cares."

Make growth issues a part of several conversations over time, not just a one-time thing. To say, "Whew, I had the tough talk with her about why she is single and not dating," is a good step. But most growth issues will require checking in. Take the long view and make your relationship a safe place to continually monitor growth and change.

We all need a little nudge in our friendships. Don't avoid them; make them a normal part of your connection. If you are consistently honest with each other in every aspect of your friendship, these nudges can become a natural and normal part of them.

Creating an Honest Environment

Most BFs truly do want permission to speak freely to each other in general, not just when a push is needed. Here are some recommendations to start.

First, become the one who models honesty about yourself, so that you both know that the truth can come out without anyone getting hurt. Bring up your own realities. Instead of always agreeing about everything, mention beliefs you have, preferences that are important to you, along with likes and dislikes. We are sometimes guilty of searching for common-alities in our friendships, so that everyone is comfortable: we both like sports, we are both into abstract art, we both have families, we both breathe air. That can become an empty experience. Being honest about yourself will give your BF freedom to define himself as well.

These questions will help you make honesty a positive part of your friendship and will also bring clarity and freedom to both of you.

- How do we rate our relationship on being honest

about ourselves: our values, beliefs, and preferences? Does the friendship welcome two different perspectives?

- How are we doing on being honest about each other? Are we both okay with bringing up something confrontational with the other person, if we feel it is important? If not, why not?

- What can we do to be connected and still be truthful? Here are some ideas:

  ❖ I'm concerned that I might hurt you and I don't want to. Can we talk about whether that's in my head or if it's reality?

  ❖ I want you to know that your feedback is vital to me. If you ever see something I'm doing that's a problem with you, or a problem in my life, I want you to tell me. You have full permission.

  ❖ What if, in every meaningful conversation, we commit to making sure that something truthful will come out? It's better to make truth an integrated part of a relationship than to have empty attachment interrupted by a truth session.

You'll find that after the initial weirdness, honesty will actually increase your connection. Things get better. Remember that honesty simply allows a person to relate to you. The more "known" we are, the more we can grow and change. That greater access puts you in a position to be transformed by God's process.

9

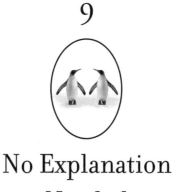

No Explanation Needed

You are surely aware of this, but you have a dark side. It may come out in a number of areas of life. It may be minor, and it may be major. But we all have aspects of ourselves that don't feel very lovable or positive. Most of the time, we don't like to look at them or be aware of them. When we do, we wish that they didn't exist, and who could blame us?

Your dark side may be a mistake you made sometime in the past that you'd like to forget. Or it may be a habit you can't put to rest that you're ashamed of. You may have a relational pattern in which you allow your fears to keep you from speaking up, or you may have one in which your tongue gets you into trouble and you alienate people from you. Whatever its nature, your dark side tends to confuse and haunt you. The apostle Paul knew this feeling quite well: "I do not understand what I do. For what I want to do I do not do, but what I hate I do" (Romans 7:15). That is the reality of the human condition. We are flawed, we are sinful, and our willpower can't erase these flaws.

In addition to your dark side, you also have a judge within you who takes hold of the mistakes you make and creates a court case out of the situation. He uses this as an opportunity to condemn and guilt you. Who isn't familiar with self-talk such as "I'm a loser," or "I'll never make it," or even "I can't stand myself"? The sting of the judge's words can make us run scared through life.

These are the times when we most need our BFs to know us and to accept us fully. This is when BFs really shine for each other. If there is anything BFs can do that is wonderful, amazing, and what we least expect, it is that they accept us for who we are, leaving shame and guilt at the door. With their compassion, they neutralize the sting of that internal judge. When your friend has no illusions about you, knows your flaws, and hangs in there with you anyway, you truly know what acceptance feels like at the deepest level. When we are accepted just as we are, we are in a position to be truly empowered to succeed and grow in life. In our best friendships, we are okay with each other not being okay.

Ideally, your BFs know all your flaws and wounds. The

more a person knows your real self at a deep level, the more whole you become. This is better than one person knowing your past, another knowing about your marriage, and another knowing your work struggles, for example. We were made to be whole, and to be made whole, in relationships. You may not have time and bandwidth to tell each other every detail of every event, but that is not necessary. Just having them know the themes and overall pictures of your reality—and loving you anyway—is generally enough.

If connection is the skill of filling each other's tanks with grace and love, acceptance is the skill of putting cleaning additives into the gasoline, so to speak. It neutralizes the dirt that has accumulated in the tank. We need both skills in our friendships.

STOPPING THE DARKNESS

Having deeply accepting friends helps us beyond the fact of being accepted by others, and then by ourselves. When our deepest relationships know us and accept us anyway, we are now free to deal with our weaknesses as a problem, rather than a condemnation. We can stop the darkness when we aren't ducking from the stings of the judge. When we aren't accepted, we are more likely to simply avoid the judgment than dig into the issue.

For example, when I work with someone struggling with a sexual addiction, we have to get through the shame stage. It is generally so intense that he can hardly bear to talk about it, understand its roots, or face it. Sexual addicts have a tendency to "get it together" prematurely. They will surrender their lives to God, commit to a church and small group, and promise they will never act out again.

This will bring a temporary relief, sort of an "it's a new day" experience. But it almost never lasts, because the issue has not been resolved. He has simply gotten rid of the shame. Until the next episode, when he becomes discouraged and feels hopeless.

It is not until he feels accepted by me as his psychologist, in addition to a few BFs who are accepting and loving and who don't allow shame, that he can truly understand that he doesn't have a sexual issue, he has a sexualized issue. The sin and sexual acting out are symptoms of a deeper issue. Often sexual problems are driven, for example, by loneliness, powerlessness, and hurt. Once he feels accepted, he can take the microscope to the dark side. He looks at his relational history, his family dynamics, how he solves problems, and how he looks at life. His acting out comes from some pain, or relational problem, or character issue, or from isolation or a sense of helplessness, to name a few causes. When the causes are identified, he can go to work and resolve the deeper issue. I have seen many people become free when they have gone through this process.

That is the power of the acceptance of a friend. It opens the door to freedom from the issues that plague us. As James put it: "Confess your sins to each other and pray for each other so that you may be healed" (James 5:16).

If acceptance wasn't important, and if we could just try harder to change our ways, we would have no need for grace, a Savior, or a redemptive process. Our BFs are an integral part of that process. I regularly tell my clients that the rate of their healing will be greatly accelerated by having great friendships where the work we are doing will be supported. Their relationships become a place where they can bring the hurts and issues with which they are grappling.

Be open about your own dark side and let your BFs walk with you through it, and be there for your BFs going through their dark sides. There may be times in which a BF won't recognize her dark side, which is an unfortunate possibility. Do everything you can to lovingly show her that she is safe, but that her choices are taking her down a destructive path, and you want to help her make the right moves.

The Real Thing

Sometimes we look to our BF to reduce our shame and self-judgment by getting us off the hook. That is, we want her to show us that our mistake was caused by someone else, or that it was all a misunderstanding. While we would find relief, it would not truly help us. The disease of the dark side would still be present. The act of labeling our screwup as an accident doesn't change its nature, and it renders us helpless to change and grow from it. True BFs accept what mistakes are really ours and love us through it.

For example, a friend of mine went through a painful and messy divorce. Fortunately, she had a very warm and accepting set of friends who walked her through the tough times. But while they were supportive and compassionate about the mistreatment she experienced from her ex, they also treated her own mistakes as reality. When she felt bad about lashing out at him or undercutting him with the kids, they didn't say, "That's OK, in comparison with what he has done to you," or "His behavior pretty much forced you to react like that." They said, "Yes, it was the wrong thing to do, and we love you and will help you not do it again." They accepted her while being honest about her actions.

DEVELOPING ACCEPTANCE

Acceptance in your best friendships can be learned and developed. It is not a one-time fact; it is a skilled process in any relationship. Here are some ways to foster that important part of your relationship.

Take the first step and do your own personal inventory and identify what dark-side issue your BF doesn't know about, or you two have skimmed over without really delving into. Bring it to her and take the risk. This is not just for you; it's for your friendship. You are giving her power to reject and judge you. But if she is the right best friend for you, she will be drawn closer to you, will know you better, and will, in turn, be more open with you about her own struggles.

Again, go further than painful situations where you've been hurt. Bring up your own poor choices and behaviors, which is where acceptance really matters.

Here are a few questions to add clarity and direction to the conversations:

- *How do you think we're doing in accepting each other's flaws and mistakes?* Do we minimize the negatives, or are we brave enough to go where the darkness is?

- *Does one of us tend to become parental, judgmental, or a moral figure when imperfections come up?* Some people get anxious and quickly denounce the problems, repeating how inappropriate the behavior is. It is most likely inappropriate, but often the person confessing is trying to get closer to God and is very aware of the inappropriateness. The moral figure is most likely dealing with anxiety and judgment in himself and is projecting it on the other person. Help that person to have the grace to listen and be accepting.

- *How can we better show acceptance to each other?* You may help each other by saying things like "I want our relationship to keep growing, and I will accept whatever you say and are, and I need that from you as well. There is no condemnation in me toward you, but if you ever feel that from me, tell me."

- After a risk: *I am feeling pretty self-judgmental now, can you tell me how you're feeling about me?* Let your friend reassure you that they are with you, and everything's okay. This will bring about even deeper connection.

The more you practice this in your best friendships, the more you will find that not only are you solving the issues you struggle with, but you are able to discuss them and open up about them with less awkwardness. You'll know you're getting somewhere when you are both able to joke about each other's dysfunction!

10

Family, Friends, and Family Friends

Suppose you said, "My sister is my best friend." That can be a wonderful thing, and you should count yourself fortunate. It means that you have family and friendship in the same package. Many people don't have that luxury. But suppose you said, "My sister and my parents and my husband are my only support system." I would say that is a problem, and something to look at.

I was counseling Rick and Jennifer, who were dealing with intimacy and connection problems. Jennifer, an accountant by profession, saw Rick, who owned a small manufacturing firm, as distant and inaccessible. He was, in her experience, emotionally unavailable. For his part, Rick saw Jennifer as clingy and somewhat insatiable. He felt that he could not do enough for her to make her feel loved and secure.

When I work with couples, sometimes both people contribute evenly to the problem and sometimes one person is contributing significantly more. As I worked with this couple, I saw that they weren't right in the middle. Rick did have tendencies to withdraw and not share his feelings; however, he was aware of this and was working on opening up. Rick was making changes to be more connected, relational, and intimate. But though these were real issues, they were more relational misdemeanors than felonies.

Jennifer's end of things was a bit more serious. She loved Rick, but was also dependent on him in ways that weren't good for either of them. When he wanted to go out with friends, Jennifer felt rejected. When he didn't spend most of his time at home communicating with her and needed to go watch TV or read for awhile, she felt unloved and alone. She was not being mean or selfish. In her heart, Jennifer simply and truly felt that way. It was as if Rick's choices to be away from her—within the home or outside of the home—were signs that he did not truly care.

I asked Jennifer who her closest relationships were, and she replied, "My family and a few other friends."

Rick interrupted: "That's not really true. It's much more about your family than your friends. You really would rather be with them than with our friends when we go out."

Jennifer argued the point for a bit before admitting,

"Okay, I'm closer to my family than my friends. You're saying that's sick or something?"

I said, "No, it's not sick at all. It's just unfinished."

"What does that mean?" Jennifer asked.

"It means that our family is the laboratory where we learn about friendships. We find out about our tastes, preferences, interests, and styles from our family, and that affects our choices all throughout life. But if we never bring non-family members into the inner circle, we are missing out."

"I don't think I'm missing out on anything," Jennifer said. "My family is very close and supportive."

"No doubt," I said. "But there are two problems in what you are describing. First, we all need the cross-pollination of lots of other types of people to be as healthy and developed as we can be. Your family can't bring you experiences with every type of music, sport, career, hobby, worship style, or restaurant. You are limiting your own growth, and you are operating as a closed system instead of an open one. Second, this is why you are smothering Rick and your marriage. I think you are afraid of his needs for autonomy and some space, and you interpret them as a lack of love and interest. They aren't that at all. Rick isn't the best connector in the world, and he is working on that. But his needs for space are for him and not against you."

My first point was a little abstract, I think, and Jennifer

didn't react to it. But as she thought about the second one, she began to tear up. I asked what the emotion was about. She said, "I'm afraid I am boring him, and he is getting restless."

Rick then weighed in: "I don't feel that at all. I am more in love with you than ever, and I'm not going anywhere." That reassured her somewhat.

Then I said, "Rick is crazy about you, right? So the problem is that you were raised in a family that emphasized closeness and avoided the outside world."

That triggered several childhood memories for Jennifer, such as how her mother would say things like, "Friends come and go, but you'll always have family," and "The world is a strange place, and who can you trust but family?" Family dominated everything, including meals, evenings, weekends, vacations, and holidays. They discouraged sleepovers. And if Jennifer ever had a real disagreement with something her parents wanted, such as the time she wanted to go to a movie with a friend instead of spending time with them, they would withdraw and be hurt, as if she was abandoning them.

What we began to work on was for Jennifer to be able to assert her natural needs for autonomy, choices, and her own voice, while still feeling loved and supported. This was new for her, but she became pretty excited about the process. She began to be less afraid and insecure. She challenged Rick's thinking and felt freer to disagree with him. Finally, she began feeling desires to have some new close friends, people she could relate to. It wasn't that she cared any less about her parents and siblings, but she wanted more outside contact, more freshness, more external energy sources. And when she began deepening a few relationships of this sort, Jennifer was finally able to say to Rick, "Sorry I've made you feel guilty about having friends and outside interests. I get it now."

CREATED TO EXPAND

God designed you to expand your horizons in many ways. You were made to increase and grow. This includes developing your character strengths, establishing an identity, finding your mission and talents, and setting up your own social support system. The family is the original place that starts this growth process. But it is not the final one. You were created to expand out of it: "For this reason a man will leave his father and mother and be united to his wife, and they will become one flesh" (Genesis 2:24). Family equips you, and hopefully launches you, and then you find people to be with, grow with, and find purpose with. That is the grand design. It forms a life of connectedness, confidence, and a desire to explore and grow emotionally, personally, relationally, and in task and mission. The expansion is to continue all through life, which is what happens with people who have had this sort of background and process.

Unfortunately, some families discourage this process and the individual never truly leaves home. Sometimes, as in Jennifer's case, the family is afraid of anything outside the family, so they discourage autonomy. Sometimes they are needy and require the child to take care of them emotionally, to be the strong one—the glue that holds the family together— because they are so broken themselves. Sometimes they hamstring the child by not providing the tools for growth, so that they are forever linked to home. However this happens, the process breaks down, and the progression from family to friends doesn't work well. If you have experienced any of these, get some help—a growth group, a mentor, a pastor, a therapist. Get assistance in finishing the work of successfully leaving home. Otherwise, you will lose a great deal of potential and joy that is available to you in life.

If, like Jennifer, you feel no need for nonfamily BFs, consider the possibility that this is a problem, that there is unfinished development and potential inside you that will require new relationships. Try to find that restlessness inside that says, "It's a big world out there with some great people," instead of, "But they know me and it's comfortable and there's no place like home." Love your home, love your family, but you were designed to also let nonfamily members into the deeper recesses of your heart and life. Jennifer had friends. But family was in the deepest and most special place inside. When she let others into that space, life became better. You are not being disloyal, nor are you abandoning your family. You are bringing more life inside your own life.

Both Sides

As I mentioned at the beginning of the chapter, you are fortunate if you have close friends who are also family. You have the advantage of someone who has it all with you: mutual attraction, shared values, and a shared long-term history. It can be a wonderful connection of great meaning and joy.

Unfortunately, it doesn't happen for many people. Sometimes it is about the family, and sometimes it is about the individual. On one side, for example, a family's stance toward life, growth, or relationships can be so toxic that it's impossible for the person to be unguarded and open with them. For example, a family may reject the person who wants to be truthful about problems in the system such as disconnection, control, alcoholism, or even, in severe cases, abuse. They will, in effect, disown the person, or at least that part of them, with the implied message of "Don't bring that opinion here." Or they may simply not be interested in the person as a person in her own right. I remember a CEO I worked with whose parents expected him to be a minister. He headed that way until he found his passion for business and changed his career trajectory. His parents said to him, "How can we tell our friends at church about this?" the implication being that he had let them down.

Whether it is about a lack of interest or something more rejecting, sometimes we have to settle for less intimacy and closeness than we would have originally wanted. That is a sad reality. It may mean having some sort of relationship, such as a friendly casualness, but you may have to accept that the requirements of a BF are not forthcoming on the other end.

On the other hand, it is also a problem when a person shuns the family and does not attempt to work things out or reconcile with them, not giving them a second or third chance to become closer. Unfortunately, this happens in the counseling world too often. The individual will get in touch with negative things that have happened in his family, and, instead of going through the process of forgiving, healing, grieving, and attempting to reconcile, he will simply take off in a permanent disconnection from the family. He becomes stuck in a protest against the wrongs done to him. I have seen this happen for years, even when the family tries to apologize, change, and work things out. This is sad, as there are only a very small percentage of families that are severely toxic. With most cases of this prolonged distance, the problem is that the individual has stayed in the protest for too long and, at a deeper level, has not given up the desire for the family to be different. He will often blame all of his present failures and struggles on the family. In those cases, he needs a counselor who will empathize with the actual sins against him; help him heal, forgive, grieve, and let go; and also push him toward more responsibility for his life, and more accountability for his own choices.

I have a good friend, Sean, whose son, Jeremy, is in his thirties and is himself a husband and a father. Sean made some mistakes as a dad with Jeremy. He was somewhat distant and unavailable and too critical. However, he saw the error of his ways and felt great remorse about these matters. He had several heartfelt conversations with Jeremy to apologize and make things right. He did everything he could think of to reconcile. Basically, he wanted to change things and establish a deep friendship between the two of them as adults. But Jeremy will have nothing to do with Sean. He has not had a successful career and will not look at his own poor choices, but only at Sean's parenting of him.

Ironically, Sean is an accomplished mentor who could offer Jeremy great direction and help him turn things around, as he has with many others. But Jeremy has no interest. Sean has had to learn to live with the distance, though it hurts terribly. He waits and keeps the door open for any move Jeremy might make, though he has had to move on and stay connected to his own group of friends. But it is a real object lesson: if this family relationship could become a friendship, the potential for both connection and success would be incredible.

BOTH-AND

The ideal scenario for family friends is both-and—have BFs within in your family and outside of it. It is not either-or as in the cases of Jennifer and Sean. Do all you can to befriend those in your family who will be the kind of friends described in this book. And as the apostle Paul reminds us, "If it is possible, as far as it depends on you, live at peace with everyone" (Romans 12:18). You are only half of the equation. You can't force this with those who are not interested. Still, make the effort and go the extra mile. But beyond that, make sure you are connected to people outside the comfort zone of family. They will actually make the family relationships better and richer, as health only adds to health. When you can have a great dinner with your brother or sister and a couple of close friends, and everyone likes everyone else, that can be a peak experience for you and for them as well.

Conclusion:
The Power of BFs

I want to leave you with a challenge: be aware of the power of your best friendships, and be aware that this power can be both positive and negative. Power is simply the ability to make something change, be it the power of electricity or politics or relationships. By definition, your BFs wield power with you, and you with them. They matter. Their opinions matter. What they say to you and how they feel and behave toward you matter. I don't mean this in some dominating way. It is just a reality that those closest to us make the greatest difference with us, and that difference can be a life-changing and life-improving direction for you. That is the positive power of BFs. Your best friends can help you become a healthier, happier, and better person by how they respond to you.

BFs also have negative power as well. A close friend can harm and wound you, unfortunately, and that happens sometimes. People are surprised by a BF relationship in which the person becomes judgmental or deceptive, for example, and it seems out of the blue. It may be that the individual simply didn't give the relationship her best that day. Or, if it is some darker character pattern, it may be that something came out that you weren't aware was inside. Whatever the cause, negative power is unavoidable, because it is your very vulnerability to that person that gives her that power. You have given her the key to the vault. She knows and has access to all of you. Those who have the key can hurt us the most. If she didn't possess it, the negative power would not exist.

Suppose you are at a stoplight and, for no good reason, the person in the lane next to you yells that you're a horrible person. That would have some effect. You might wonder if something is wrong with your driving, or if the person is having a bad day, or if he is crazy. But beyond it being a good story to tell that week, that's about the extent of it. But suppose your closest friend said you are a horrible person. That would be a problem. You would feel horrible that she thinks you are horrible. You would wonder what reality was. You would feel a hurt inside that someone you have let in so deeply, thinks so poorly of you. You would want to have several discussions with her, and other people, to figure this out and get past it. There is nothing wrong with that sort of vulnerability. It is just the reality of having deeper relationships. You can't have a BF without the potential of that sort of negative power. That is the challenge.

I started this book with the story of Rachel and how BFs were lifelines to her. While we may not be in Rachel's circumstances, we all need the lifelines. A great deal of your life choices and directions will be influenced by the power of your BFs. When it is time to give them feedback, choose your words carefully because they matter a great deal to your BFs. When it is time to hear feedback, know that you are hearing something that has great importance. Pay attention to the care of your BFs. They can't be overestimated.

Be a person who cares about many people, but has invested deeply in a few. Like Proverbs says, "A man of many companions may come to ruin, but there is a friend who sticks closer than a brother" (Proverbs 18:24). Your life will show the fruit both today and tomorrow.

God bless you.

Dr. John Townsend
Newport Beach, California
2011

STUDY
GUIDE

Introduction

HAVING GOOD FRIENDS

1. Circle any of the following descriptions that match your experience of best friends, or add your own description at the end. Then, next to each applicable statement, write the name(s) or initials of the friend(s) you immediately thought of when you first read those words.

   - Safe places where I can be myself.

   - The few people I can be comfortable with.

   - The ones I go to when I need support.

   - Know and accept all of me.

   - Have walked with me through the seasons of life (marriage, childrearing, loss, etc.).

- I have found God in a deeper way through them.

- Helped me through tough times.

- Made my life more meaningful.

-

-

2. Why is it significant that when Jesus was in Gethsemane, just hours away from the cross, he looked not only to his heavenly Father but also to his closest earthly friends—Peter, James, and John? (See Matthew 26:36–38.)

3. Think for a moment about a few of those special people on your BF list and ask yourself these questions:

   a. *In what specific areas of life could my best friend and I do better for each other?* For example, is your connection focused too much on one specific topic—say, parenting, marriage, or dating? What important areas—like physical health, family of origin, spiritual values, or finances—don't get discussed? How will you begin to dig into those additional facets of life to enrich your friendship?

b. *What risk might we need to take to make our relationship even better?*

BEING A GOOD FRIEND

4. Prayerfully read the following "one anothers" selected from the more than fifty that are mentioned in the New Testament. Which two or three of these do you most need to work on? (If you're not sure, a true friend will undoubtedly be able to tell you!)

Choose one of these traits and the friendship in which you will cultivate it this week. Then make a plan, and make sure it happens!

- *Mark 9:50* "Be at peace with each other."

- *Romans 12:10* "Be devoted to one another. . . . Honor one another above yourselves."

- *Romans 14:13* "Stop passing judgment on one another."

- *Galatians 5:13* "Serve one another in love."

- *Galatians 6:2* "Carry each other's burdens."

- *Ephesians 4:32* "Be kind and compassionate to one another, forgiving each other, just as in Christ God forgave you."

- *Ephesians 5:21* "Submit to one another out of reverence for Christ."

- *Colossians 3:9* "Do not lie to each other."

- *1 Thessalonians 5:11* "Encourage one another and build each other up."

- *Hebrews 10:24–25* "Spur one another on toward love and good deeds."

- *James 5:16* "Confess your sins to each other and pray for each other."

5. In Mark 2:1–12, the good friends of the paralytic brought him before Jesus so the Lord could bless and heal the man. Which of your BFs especially need(s) Jesus' touch of healing, hope, or encouragement today? Bring those friends before Jesus in prayer.

1

Fs, BFs, and BFFs

Having Good Friends

1. At the DNA level, a friendship must have three elements: knowing, liking, and presence. Why is each of these essential to a healthy, life-giving relationship?

2. To whom, if anyone, have you handed over the key to the vault of your life? What did you learn from that experience?

3. Look at the list below. Which kinds of information about yourself do you find most difficult to share? Which kinds are most difficult for you to listen to when someone else is sharing? Why are those topics tough for you?

Dreams	Hurts	Vision for Life
Secrets	Feelings	Sins
Core Values	Mistakes	Strengths
The Past	Heartaches	

4. Some good friends are friends for a season. Comment on the positives and negatives of that reality. What factors contribute to making someone a forever friend?

5. Can you have or should you have more than one best friend? Why or why not? And what do you think about having best friends of the opposite sex?

BEING A GOOD FRIEND

6. For each of your best friends, consider what percentage of that relationship is based on knowing? on liking? on presence? What practical steps can you take to strengthen each element of those friendships?

7. If you have a best friend of the opposite sex, what precautions are you taking to keep it appropriate—or what safeguards might be good to implement?

2

The Accidental Necessity

HAVING GOOD FRIENDS

1. Who in your life would you categorize as a companion? as a best friend? Why did the people on the "Best Friend" list make the cut? Why do you think each person sensed you were open to healthy, new relationships?

2. When, if ever, has a best friend helped a struggle of yours come to light and then kept it from becoming a bigger issue? Why are BFs able to have that kind of significant impact on us?

3. If you are married, when has your time with a best friend—or your spouse's time with a best friend—improved your marriage? If you're single, has a dating relationship ever benefited from your best friend's involvement? How does spending time with a best friend not only fuel you but fuel your relationship with "significant others" as well?

4. We all need to be transparent with someone about our inner selves, needs, mistakes, and emotions. What keeps people—or has kept you—from being vulnerable like that? What good things come with the choice to be transparent in a friendship?

BEING A GOOD FRIEND

5. What fears of being vulnerable do you have, if any? What would facing those fears in the arena of friendship look like? Be specific about actions you could take in an effort to overcome those fears.

6. What will you do with one or two of your BFs this week to intentionally care for and maintain those relationships? Note how the friendship benefits when you take those purposeful actions.

3

Life Is Better When
We Are Hanging Out Together

HAVING GOOD FRIENDS

1. Friendship has two parts: liking and connecting. What happens if you have one without the other?

2. When, if ever, have you grown to like someone because you learned his or her story? For what current relationship does that experience encourage you?

3. To deepen our connection with a friend, we need to act in ways that foster trust and openness. Brainstorm some specific ways to do that—some of which will probably require you to take the initial risk of going deeper in that friendship.

4. When have you seen someone being drawn to another person for less-than-healthy reasons—or when have you experienced that yourself? Why does such attraction happen? What steps can we take to prevent such attachments?

Being a Good Friend

5. One way we come to have good friends is by being a good friend. So do unto others at some point this week and try at least one of the following:

- Make a no-purpose phone call.

- Take the lead in bringing up your own needs for grace, validation, acceptance, understanding, or safety with a friend.

- Go deeper in a conversation by sharing how you feel, not just how you think. Mention what concerns you, frustrates you, or saddens you.

Now consider: What difference did that action make?

4

The Time Investment

Having Good Friends

1. Why are both quality time and quantity time essential to best friendships?

2. Children develop a sense of being loved and secure when they have "internalized" parents who were consistently warm and loving. This emotional pic-

ture of Mom and Dad cheers the kids on and comforts them in times of stress. Who in your life has made that life-giving contribution to your soul even if your parents didn't? Give an example of when an internalized BF helped you take a difficult step.

3. *"Best friend* should be an earned title rather than an honorary one." Do you agree or disagree with this statement? Why?

4. Why is proximity as important as time when it comes to preserving and strengthening a best friendship? In what ways can BFs compensate for a lack of proximity?

Being a Good Friend

5. Look at some of your most important relationships and think about how you're doing in the areas of being caught up on life events, connected emotionally, and close enough to be able to speak and hear truth. Which friend(s) do you need to see more often? What change in your schedule over the next seven days are you going to make in order to see someone you haven't seen for a while?

5

BFs in a Facebook World

HAVING GOOD FRIENDS

1. What percentage of your contact with your BFs is through digital connections such as texting, email, and social media like Facebook and Twitter? Are those connections making your best friendships stronger? Why or why not?

2. Why has good, old-fashioned face-to-face communication not yet been matched by technology? Specifically, what aspects of communication are lost when we communicate via technology? Give an example of how, without those nonverbal cues, our words can have a completely opposite meaning.

3. Think about the downside of digital connections. When has something negative or confrontational seemed much worse when you (or your recipient) read it, simply because it wasn't communicated in person? In what ways have you—and/or someone you've connected with via text, email, or social media—been able to hide parts of yourself you didn't want known or create parts of yourself that didn't exist?

4. Why is it important to first clarify for ourselves what we're thinking and feeling before going to BFs? Describe a time when a BF helped you clarify your reality *after* you had already done some reflecting on your own. You may also be able to tell of a time when you went prematurely to a BF, adopted her reality, and later regretted it.

Being a Good Friend

5. What can we do to stand strong against the temptation to hide behind technology or not be real?

6. While digital communication can definitely help you stay in contact with your BFs, it is also important to make sure you're connecting with people in person. How balanced is your life right now? Are you connecting face-to-face with new friends? with long-time friends? Be honest with yourself about where, if at all, you are hiding behind a Facebook image or text messages. What step will you take this week to be more balanced in your face-to-face vs. technological connections?

6

Speed Dial

HAVING GOOD FRIENDS

1. When have you experienced the reality that the high points are more joyful when shared with a BF? And when has a low point in life seemed less low, less hopeless, because you had a BF by your side? Why do you think such timely connecting with a BF has these effects?

2. Validation has to do with knowing that your own experience matters to someone else. When has a BF's validation been exactly what you needed when you needed it? Explain how such validation makes us "more of ourselves."

3. When have you needed a BF to simply be present with you? When have you needed a BF to help you move on from being in shock, make wise choices, and develop a plan of action? Comment on what your BF provided for you when you were in crisis.

4. Who do you have on your speed dial, either literally or figuratively, when you need to vent? Why that person? What does that BF offer even when you're in a seemingly impossible situation?

BEING A GOOD FRIEND

5. In what best friendship(s), if any, are you purposely keeping quiet about a current challenge, disappointment, or hurt? Explain in your own words why such attempts actually make us high maintenance—and then plan to get together with that BF so you can let him or her know what's going on and allow that person to support you.

7

What Matters Most

HAVING GOOD FRIENDS

1. When, if ever, have you realized that you and a BF had diametrically opposed values and chosen to distance yourself from him or her? Explain your decision.

2. *Core values* are those general truths—like love, responsibility, freedom, and forgiveness—that you allow to guide all areas of your life. What are your three or four most important core values? How do you determine if your BFs share those core values?

3. *Context values* are your beliefs about how to conduct specific areas of your life—such as your finances, family, career, health, and political views. In what context values do you and your BFs differ? Why can differences in context values be beneficial? What personal growth, for instance, have you experienced because of such differences?

4. If you are a Christian, do you believe that all your BFs should be Christians as well? Why or why not? Does this limit the degree of intimacy you can experience? In what ways might this difference enrich a friendship?

BEING A GOOD FRIEND

5. With which of your BFs are you intentionally or unnecessarily staying separate in your context values? Explain. Which core values are keeping you deeply connected to which BFs? If you find large differences in the core values you and a BF have, talk about those values and determine how to preserve and even strengthen your friendship.

8

Permission to Speak the Truth

Having Good Friends

1. Why is other people's truthfulness critical to our growth? Give an example from your own life: when did someone's words of truth spark some kind of growth in you?

2. Best friends are truthful about themselves and truthful about each other. How can a BF's honesty about you be valuable?

3. When have you been "truthed without grace"—and when have you perhaps spoken truth without grace? What lessons did you learn from those experiences?

4. Best friends are completely honest with each other and push each other to grow. Are you and your BF(s) too careful with each other? Why isn't this a problem—or why might this be the case?

5. What can you say to help a BF—or yourself—see that truth does not mean condemnation but can instead be a gift of great love?

BEING A GOOD FRIEND

6. Model honesty about yourself with one of your BFs. One day this week, ask a BF to help you see areas in yourself where you're not growing, things you're doing that aren't healthy, blind spots you aren't aware of, and even areas of potential that you may not see. To encourage yourself to have this conversation, list three or four benefits to this kind of honesty within your best friendships.

9

No Explanation Needed

1. In our best friendships, we are okay with each other being *not* okay. Which BFs have accepted your dark side? Which BFs have helped you both recognize and learn to ignore your internal judge? Which specific flaws, sins, and mistakes of yours is a BF well aware of but accepts and loves you anyway?

2. Why is it necessary to deal with our weaknesses as *problems* rather than a cause for *condemnation?*

3. How is a BF's acceptance helpful in identifying the cause of our sin and resolving that deeper issue rather than merely dealing with the symptom?

4. What integral part of God's redemptive process can BFs play? Ideally, talk about when a BF has been significant to God's work in your life.

BEING A GOOD FRIEND

5. The first step in developing greater acceptance in a friendship is to do your own personal inventory. Take that step this week, identifying a dark-side issue, a poor choice, or an unhealthy behavior that your BF doesn't know about or is only generally aware of. Then share it with the person and admit: "I'm beating myself up. I need to know I'm okay with you." You might even conduct an acceptance inventory together by discussing: *How do you think we're doing in accepting each other's flaws and mistakes? How can we better show each other acceptance?*

10

Family, Friends, and Family Friends

1. Your family is the laboratory where you learn about friendships. What did relationships with your parents and/or siblings teach you about having friends? about being a friend?

2. As important as family relationships are, we all need the cross-pollination of other types of people if we are to be as healthy and developed as we can be. What have you learned about yourself and about this big world—with all its variety—that you wouldn't have experienced if you had stayed in the laboratory of the family?

3. Why might a person's lack of desire for nonfamily BFs indicate some unfinished development and/or untapped potential? Why is this a problem?

4. Are you blessed to have close friends who are family? If so, what contributed to these rich relationships? If not, consider honestly—and learn from your conclusions—whether the reason is more you or more the family system.

5. Maybe your family members are not close friends because of a lack of forgiveness. If that's the case, what is keeping you from entering the process of forgiving, healing, grieving, and attempting to reconcile?

BEING A GOOD FRIEND

6. The ideal scenario for family friends is both-and: it's having BFs both within your family and outside of it. What can you do to better befriend someone in your family? Choose a family member, select one of the steps you just brainstormed, and make an intentional effort in the next week or so to more deeply connect with him or her.

Conclusion:
The Power of BFs

HAVING GOOD FRIENDS

1. Why is it important to be aware of the power—both positive and negative—of your best friendships?

2. What four or five examples come to mind right away when you think about how your BFs have changed

your life? Have all of those changes been for the better? Why or why not?

3. Comment on the wisdom of this statement: "We all need the lifelines of best friends. Be a person who cares about many people, but has invested deeply in a few." How easy or difficult is it for you to follow this advice—and why?

4. What have you most appreciated about this book's discussion of BFFs?

BEING A GOOD FRIEND

Go back and look at each of the "Being a Good Friend" exercises that you have been challenged with in the course of this study. Which two or three helped you the most? Now brainstorm how you can continue to build on those action steps over the long-term.

Notes

Introduction

1. Tom Rath, *Vital Friends: The People You Can't Afford to Live Without* (New York: Gallup Press, 2006), Kindle edition, chapter 3: "Better than Prozac?" and Farouk Mookadam and Heather M. Arthur, "Social Support and Its Relationship to Morbidity and Mortality After Acute Myocardial Infarction," *Archives of Internal Medicine* 164 (2004): 1514–18.

2. Alina Tugend, "Peeking at the Negative Side of High School Popularity," *New York Times*, June 19, 2010, B6.

Chapter 3

1. I have written more extensively on connection in my book *Loving People: How to Love and Be Loved* (Nashville: Thomas Nelson, 2007).

Chapter 4

1. Robert Lee Holtz, "The Really Smart Phone," *Wall Street Journal*, April 23, 2011.

Chapter 8

1. Henry Cloud and John Townsend, *Boundaries: When to Say Yes, When to Say No, to Take Control of Your Life* (Grand Rapids: Zondervan, 1992).
2. Jim Collins, *Good to Great* (New York: Harper Business Books, 2001).

John Townsend is a business consultant, psychologist, and relational expert. He has written or cowritten twenty-six books, including the two million-unit bestseller *Boundaries, Leadership Beyond Reason,* and *Handling Difficult People.* For more than twenty years Dr. Townsend has engaged with leaders, organizations, and individuals around the globe, offering them life-changing solutions to their problems. He is cohost of the nationally syndicated radio talk show *NewLifeLive*—heard in 180 markets with three million listeners—and has been interviewed on venues such as Fox News television and published in magazines such as *Personal Excellence* and *Leadership Journal.* He is also a regular columnist for *Christian Coaching Today* magazine.

The cofounder and director of a health-care company for ten years, with operations in thirty-five cities in the western U.S., it was here that Townsend learned the strategies for change and success that he now employs in his coaching and writing. Dr. Townsend works with leaders and organizations by providing team and executive coaching and corporate consulting, and by giving conference presentations. He also conducts his own Leadership Coaching Program, as well as the Ultimate Leadership Workshop.

He is both a visiting professor at Dallas Seminary and clinical director of the American Association of Christian Counselors, and conducts the One Week Intensive training experience for counselors. In addition, Townsend is on the board of directors of the New Canaan Society—an organization dedicated to the spiritual and personal growth of Christian businessmen—and is active on the board of Mustard Seed Ranch, a residential program for abused children.

A resident of Newport Beach, California, Townsend and his wife, Barbi, have two sons.

DR. JOHN TOWNSEND'S LEADERSHIP COACHING PROGRAM
For Leaders Who Want to Achieve Their Potential

Best-selling author, psychologist, and leadership consultant Dr. John Townsend conducts The Leadership Coaching Program, which is based on his own research and design. This program offers a unique approach to accelerating leadership and business performance that produces value-add and tangible results. Using a team format with a maximum of ten members per team, John personally conducts programs in Newport Beach (CA), Dallas, and Indianapolis. As part of this team, you'll have a unique opportunity to spend face-to-face training time with Dr. Townsend. He'll work with you to develop powerful strategies and will help you measure your personal progress and growth with individually designed homework assignments, allowing you to take what you have experienced and apply it to your context. Experience the next-level training and growth you are after, to produce the results you want. Dr. Townsend's Leadership Coaching Program will provide the direction, answers, and motivation you need for success.

Contact info:
assistant@drtownsend.com
www.drtownsend.com
949-249-2398

Testimonials
"The Leadership Coaching Program experience with Dr. Townsend was a process of self-discovery that enhanced my leadership capabilities and, at the same time, offered me a unique opportunity for personal growth."

Walt Rose, Emeritus Co-Chairman of the Board,
Children's Hospital, Los Angeles

"In the Leadership Coaching Program, I gained insight into myself and others that will benefit me forever."

Glenn Hansen,
Former Executive, Best Buy

WORTHY
PUBLISHING

IF YOU LIKED THIS BOOK . . .

- Tell your friends by going to: www.howtobeabestfriendforever.com and clicking "LIKE"

  - Share the video book trailer by posting it on your Facebook page

  - Head over to our Facebook page, click "LIKE" and post a comment regarding what you enjoyed about the book

  - Tweet "I recommend reading #HowToBeABestFriendForever by @drjohntownsend@Worthypub"

- Hashtag: #BestFriendForever

- Subscribe to our newsletter by going to http://worthypublishing .com/about/subscribe.php

WORTHY PUBLISHING
FACEBOOK PAGE

WORTHY PUBLISHING
WEBSITE